Understanding Secular Religions

BOOKS BY JOSH MCDOWELL

Reasons Skeptics Should Consider Christianity

Prophecy: Fact or Fiction

More Than a Carpenter

Evidence That Demands a Verdict

Evidence Growth Guide: The Uniqueness of Christianity

More Evidence That Demands a Verdict

The Resurrection Factor

The Resurrection Factor Growth Guide

Answers to Tough Questions

Givers, Takers and Other Kinds of Lovers

Handbook of Today's Religions—Understanding the Cults

Handbook of Today's Religions—Understanding the Occult

Handbook of Today's Religions—Understanding Non-Christian Religions

Handbook of Today's Religions—Understanding Secular Religions

Josh McDowell
& Don Stewart

HANDBOOK OF TODAY'S RELIGIONS

Understanding Secular Religions

CAMPUS CRUSADE FOR CHRIST
Published by
HERE'S LIFE PUBLISHERS, INC.
San Bernardino, California 92402

HANDBOOK OF TODAY'S RELIGIONS
Understanding Secular Religions
by Josh McDowell
and Don Stewart

A Campus Crusade for Christ Book
Published by
HERE'S LIFE PUBLISHERS, INC.
P. O. Box 1576, San Bernardino, CA 92402

ISBN 0-86605-093-0
HLP product No. 402859

Printed in the United States of America

FOR MORE INFORMATION, WRITE:

L.I.F.E.—P. O. Box A399, Sydney South 2000, Australia
Campus Crusade for Christ of Canada—Box 368, Abbottsford, B.C., V25 4N9, Canada
Campus Crusade for Christ—103 Friar Street, Reading RGI IEP, Berkshire, England
Campus Crusade for Christ—28 Westmoreland St., Dublin 2, Ireland
Lay Institute for Evangelism—P. O. Box 8786, Auckland 3, New Zealand
Life Ministry—P. O. Box/Bus 91015, Auckland Park 2006, Republic of So. Africa
Campus Crusade for Christ, Int'l—Arrowhead Springs, San Bernardino, CA 92414, U.S.A.

"Beloved, believe not every spirit, but try the spirits whether they are of God, because many false prophets are gone out into the world" (1 John 4:1 KJV).

Table of Contents

Introduction

Understanding Secular Religions

In this volume of our series, we present brief discussions of some of the most dynamic secular alternatives to Christianity which are available today. These alternatives are not strictly religious since they have no belief in God or the supernatural, and involve no form of worship or liturgy. That is why we have labeled them *secular.*

However, they are religious in the sense that they are more or less unified comprehensive world views which seek to explain the "why" of existence. Because they have their own creeds, their own "scriptures," their own "clergy," and their own closely knit groups, we have labeled them *religions*.

The First Three Volumes

This series, *Handbook of Today's Religions,* has now grown to four volumes. The first volume, *Understanding the Cults,* deals with some of the most prominent cults in contemporary society. A "cult" is a religious group that claims to be compatible with historic and biblical Christianity but which denies it in either significant essential doctrinal or methodological points. The second volume, *Understanding the Occult,* deals with that area of religious belief which is primarily in direct opposition to biblical Christianity. This religious belief can range from a comprehensive theology such as some forms of Satanism to the deceitful and fraudulent practices of pseudo-mediums. Volume three, *Understanding Non-Christian Religions*, takes as its topic the major world religions which do not claim to represent biblical Christianity. We discuss the ancient religions, such as Hinduism and Judaism, as well as the newer resurrections of ancient thought, such as Buddhism's Nichiren Shoshu. This fourth volume, *Understanding Secular Religions*, presents secular alternatives to Christian belief.

Our Topics

In this volume we do not presume to have exhausted all of the secular alternatives to Christianity. However, we do believe that the four movements we have chosen to discuss are representative of those alternatives.

Two of our topics are loosely organized and consist primarily of ideas rather than existing as full-blown belief systems. These two, *existentialism* and *atheism* (which includes agnosticism and skepticism), are more properly types of philosophical thought rather than comprehensive movements. However, they still challenge the Christian world view and demand an almost religious commitment. Our other two topics, *Marxism* and *Secular Humanism*, appear to be complete world views and belief systems. They are the secular substitutes for Christianity and more nearly fit the traditional definition of religion.

The Scope of Our Study

Whole libraries are built to the honor of secular religions, as we have defined them. For instance one could read a different book each day for several years on Marxism alone. There are those, both within and without the camp of biblical Christianity, who have spent their entire careers studying and commenting upon such subjects. We do not pretend that we have such expertise; rather, we cite those scholars who are recognized generally as authorities.

Neither do we pretend that this one short overview will deal comprehensively with the four secular systems. Our goal in presenting this volume to the Christian public is to provide the Christian with enough background in the subjects under discussion so that he can understand the basic tenets of each system. We have chosen to present, therefore, summaries of the teachings of the relevant philosophies rather than present voluminous quotes from the philosophies themselves. Following the background, we have given ways to think about the subject from a biblical and rational perspective. We are more concerned with principles than with details, with general biblical responses than with meticulous critiques. This book has enough information to give the reader a Christian perspective on humanism, atheism, agnosticism, skepticism, Marxism, and existentialism.

We hope that this review will whet the appetite of the reader and encourage him to look to the volumes listed in our extensive bibliographies for further information.

If we give Christians a biblical perspective on the subject of secular religion, or enable Christians to think in a rational and biblical manner as they respond to the challenges of secular religion, we will consider our task successfully accomplished.

We especially would like to thank Robert and Gretchen Passantino for their advice, which was actively solicited on all four volumes, and for their considerable help with the chapters on Marxism and atheism in this volume. We would also like to thank our publishers for their close cooperation in this project.

Chapter One

Atheism, Agnosticism, and Skepticism

While it might seem odd at first to include atheism, agnosticism, and skepticism in a series on religion, these three systems of thought should be addressed here. Religion is sometimes defined as whatever about which a man is deeply concerned,[1] and it is to such concerns that we now turn. Everyone, even the nontheist, attempts to make sense of and explain the reality around him. While those who believe in some form of God attribute this world's existence in some way to that God (or gods); the atheist, agnostic, and skeptic form an alternative naturalistic explanation for this world.

Since our space is limited, we usually will refer to the three views as one, recognizing the great overlap among them. Where their distinctions are important we will point them out. After defining the three terms we will review briefly the history of the nontheistic (apart from God) movement. Then we will discuss five kinds of objections which represent most of the arguments brought by nonbelievers against a belief in God. These five objections include problems in the areas of language, knowledge, moral concepts, scientific method, and logic. Since this is to be a survey of nontheistic religions, and not a presentation of Christianity, we will not present

---

[1]Richard Purtill, *Reason to Believe*, Grand Rapids, MI: William B. Eerdmans Publishing Company, 1974, p. 10.

systematic proofs for the existence of God, but we will present short theistic resolutions to the five problems mentioned. We have included the names of the major philosophers whose writings would be helpful in understanding these areas of belief.

Definitions

Atheism

The word *atheism* comes from the Greek prefix *a* (no or non-) and the noun *theos* (god or God). An *atheist* is one who believes that there exists positive evidence that there is no God. To the atheist, all of existence can be explained naturally rather than supernaturally. An atheist is convinced that all religious belief, evidence, and faith are false.

Popular authors and philosophy professors William and Mabel Sahakian explain it as follows:

> Unlike Agnostics, the Atheist takes a definite stand, arguing that proof regarding God's existence or nonexistence is available, but that the evidence favors the assumption of nonexistence (William and Mabel Sahakian, *Ideas of the Great Philosophers*, New York: Harper and Row, Publishers, 1966, p. 100).

Bishop Charles Gore summarizes atheistic belief as presupposing

> that we see in the world of which we form a part no signs of anything corresponding to the mind or spirit or purposes which indisputably exist in man—no signs of a universal spirit or reason with which we can hold communion, nothing but blind and unconscious force (Charles Gore, *The Reconstruction of Belief*, London: John Murray, 1926, pp. 45,46).

Historically, *atheism* sometimes refers to a rejection of only particular gods or a particular God. Hans Schwarz informs us that

> When the Greek philosopher Anaxagoras, for instance, declared that the sun was an incandescent stone somewhat larger than the Peloponesus, he was accused of impiety or atheism and forced to leave his hometown Athens (Hans Schwarz, *The Search for God*, Minneapolis, MN: Augsburg Publishing House, 1975, p. 16).

Plato in his *Laws X* (c. 352-350 B.C.) defined two basic kinds of atheists: those who are sincerely convinced God (or gods) does not exist; and those who assert that there is no place for God (or gods) in this world. The first kind of atheist is considered moral and upright while the second kind is seen as an anarchistic (without law) threat to society.[2] Socrates may have been put to death for being this second kind of atheist. Again, Schwarz notes,

> ...when Socrates was indicted for "impiety" in 399 B.C. on grounds that he had corrupted the young and neglected the gods during worship ceremonies ordered by the city and had introduced religious novelties, he was sentenced to death and was condemned to drink the hemlock within twenty-four hours. But Socrates' position and that of other atheists was far from being atheistic in the modern sense (ibid., p. 17).

Agnosticism

Agnosticism comes from the Greek prefix *a-* (no or non-) and the noun *gnosis* (knowledge, usually by experience). An agnostic is one who believes there is insufficient evidence to prove or disprove the existence or nonexistence of God or gods. Agnostics criticize the theist and the atheist for their dogmatism and their presumption of such knowledge.

William and Mabel Sahakian say that agnosticism "refers to a neutralist view on the question of the existence of God; it is the view of the person who elects to remain in a state of suspended judgment" (Sahakian and Sahakian, *Ideas*, p. 100).

The Runes *Dictionary of Philosophy* defines agnosticism as:

> 1. (epist.) that theory of knowledge which asserts that it is impossible for man to attain knowledge of a certain subject-matter. 2. (theol.) that theory of religious knowledge which asserts that it is impossible for man to attain knowledge of God (Dagobert D. Runes, ed., *Dictionary of Philosophy*, Totowa, NJ: Littlefield, Adams & Company, 1960, 1962, p. 7).

This is complemented by Peter Angeles' *Dictionary of Philosophy*, which defines agnosticism as:

---

[2]Edith Hamilton and Huntington Cairns, eds., *Plato: The Collected Dialogues*, Princeton, NJ: Princeton University Press, 1961, pp. 1463-1465.

> 1. The belief (a) that we cannot have knowledge of God and (b) that it is impossible to prove that God exists or does not exist. 2. Sometimes used to refer to the suspension of judgment... about some types of knowledge such as about the soul, immortality, spirits, heaven, hell, extraterrestrial life (Peter Angeles, *Dictionary of Philosophy*, New York: Harper & Row, Publishers, 1981, p. 20).

There are two types of agnostics. One type says there is insufficient evidence but leaves open the possiblility of sometime obtaining enough evidence to know with certainty. The second type is convinced that it is objectively impossible for anyone to ever know with certainty the existence or non-existence of God or gods.

William and Mabel Sahakian add this distinction to their definition of agnosticism (see above):

> One group of Agnostics assumes that it merely lacks the facts necessary to form a judgment and defers any conclusion pending the acquisition of such facts; another group assumes a more dogmatic position, contending that facts are not available because it is impossible now (and will continue to be impossible) to obtain these facts—a view exemplified in Immanuel Kant's attacks upon the traditional arguments for the existence of God (Sahakian and Sahakian, *Ideas*, p. 100).

Christian authors Norman Geisler and Paul Feinberg also point out the distinction between the two kinds of agnostics:

> One form of agnosticism claims that we *do not* know if God exists; the other insists that we *cannot* know. The first we'll call "soft" and the second "hard" agnosticism. We are not here concerned about "soft" agnosticism, since it does not eliminate in principle the possibility of knowing whether God exists. It says in effect, "I do not know whether God exists but it is not impossible to know. I simply do not have enough evidence to make a rational decision on the question." We turn, then, to the "hard" form which claims that it is impossible to know whether God exists (Norman Geisler and Paul Feinberg, *Introduction to Philosophy: A Christian Perspective*, Grand Rapids, MI: Baker Book House, 1980, p. 296).

Skepticism

Skepticism is derived from the Latin *scepticus* (inquiring, reflective, doubting). The Latin in turn comes from the Greek *scepsis* (inquiry, hesitation, doubt). The

Greeks used the word to refer to a certain school of philosophical thought, the Skeptics[3] (see *History* below), who taught that because real knowledge is unattainable, one should suspend judgment on matters of truth. This meaning is carried in Runes' *Dictionary of Philosophy*:

> A proposition about a method of obtaining knowledge: that every hypothesis should be subjected to continual testing; that the only or the best or a reliable method of obtaining the knowledge of one or more of the above kinds is to doubt until something indubitable or as nearly indubitable as possible is found; that wherever evidence is indecisive, judgment should be suspended; that knowledge of all or certain kinds at some point rests on unproved postulates or assumptions (Runes, *Philosophy*, p. 278).

This is confirmed by B. A. G. Fuller's *A History of Philosophy*, where he reminds us that the "role of skepticism is to remind men that knowing with absolute certainty is impossible" (B. A. G. Fuller, *A History of Philosophy*, New York: Holt, Rinehart and Winston, 1955, vol. II, p. 581).

Peter Angeles shows in his definition of *skepticism* that there is a range of belief within the system. He writes that skepticism is:

> 1. A state of doubting. 2. A state of suspension of judgment. 3. A state of unbelief or nonbelief. Skepticism ranges from complete, total disbelief in everything, to a tentative doubt in a process of reaching certainty (Angeles, *Philosophy*, p. 258).

While skepticism is sometimes synonymous with certain definitions of agnosticism, other writers distinguish between skepticism and agnosticism as does Warren Young, who writes:

> Skepticism carries the negative attitude a step farther than agnosticism, denying the possibility of human knowledge. Truth in an objective sense is unattainable by any means within man's reach (Warren Young, *A Christian Approach to Philosophy*, Grand Rapids, MI: Baker Book House, 1954, p. 61).

---

[3] Skepticism is capitalized when used as the title of a school of philosophy; and is in lower case when used to describe a general concept.

Keeping in mind Geisler and Feinberg's two kinds of agnosticism (see above under the definition of agnosticism), their comments on the differences between agnosticism and skepticism are important. They write,

> The skeptic neither affirms nor denies God's existence. And in contrast to the (hard) agnostic, the skeptic does not say it is impossible to know. For (hard) agnosticism too is a form of dogmatism – negative dogmatism. The skeptic claims to take a much more tentative attitude toward knowledge. He is not sure whether a man can or cannot know God. In fact, the complete skeptic is not sure of anything (Geisler and Feinberg, *Philosophy*, p. 299).

Because of the overlap of definitions for atheism, agnosticism, and skepticism, it is at times difficult and even unnecessary to distinguish one's usage of the terms. What is most important to remember is that most non-religious people, while they may label themselves with one of the three terms, usually have no clear understanding of how their own views fit one category but not the others. A person may be regarded as an atheist but, in actual practice, fall under the common definition of an agnostic. Another person may be regarded as a skeptic but admit to the possibility of change to accept some universal truths. If someone questions everything, the title "skeptic" can be applied. But since certainty might be found someday it would be appropriate to be seen as an agnostic. However, if at this time that person does not believe in God, is "atheist" the proper term? While the three terms are useful to us (as in reading other philosophy works), the terms are relatively unimportant in most personal encounters. If we can establish what someone believes about knowledge, about obtaining knowledge, and about the ultimate meaning of existence, then we can deal with that person on the level at which he is comfortable. In such a situation, the label of atheist, agnostic, or skeptic is unimportant.

History

As we look at brief histories of atheism, agnosticism, and skepticism, we will reverse our order of discussion to reflect the chronological development of these three areas of philosophical thought. There have been skeptics, atheists, and agnostics throughout the history of mankind, and we will treat skepticism first, then atheism, and finally agnosticism.

Skepticism

The Greek schools of Skepticism began around 365 B.C. The first skeptic philosopher of note was Pyrrho of Elis (365-275 B.C.). The Pyrrhonic School held that skepticism was so pervasive that even their theory of skepticism was not certain. Skepticism was adopted as a way to avoid mental and emotional distress caused by conflicting data.

> ...the central idea of the early Skeptics was to avoid mental insecurity or doubt by abstaining from judgment on issues; suspension of judgment (*epoche*) became the fundamental theory of Skepticism. The policy of withholding judgment applied not only to metaphysical and logical questions, but also to value judgments pertaining to right conduct, the good, and the desirable....
>
> The Skeptics, who were called the doubters, suspenders of judgment, and inquirers, based their philosophy on the premise that since we can know nothing of ultimate reality, then such basic things are matters of indifference to us, and they must be treated as inconsequential (William Sahakian, *History of Philosophy*, New York: Harper & Row, Publishers, 1968, pp. 48,49).

A second school of Skepticism is called Academic Skepticism, or the Middle Academy. Its leaders were Arcesilaus of Pitane in Aeolia (315-241 B.C.), Carneades of Cyrene (214-129 B.C.), and Clitomachus (187-109 B.C.). The basic premise of Academic Skepticism is summarized well by Sahakian:

> The Academic Skeptics set forth the fundamental premise that they could know only one thing, namely, that nothing is knowable (ibid., pp. 49,50).

The Academics spent most of their efforts attacking the teachings of the Stoics,[4] and their presentation of Skepticism was often done in direct contrast to Stoicism. Arcesilaus stated that, while one could not know, even about ethics, one could judge probability and that, in fact, one should order his life by probability. He was followed by Carneades, who postulated three degrees of probability.

> 1. In the first place, we have mere probability, where we act

with little or no observation of simlar situations to help us, and where the chances therefore are about fifty-fifty, but seem worth taking in view of what we shall gain if we win.

2. Secondly, we have undisputed probability, where empirical observation shows us that other people have repeatedly taken the same chances successfully and to their advantage, and have never lost. Here the face-value of the probable truth and reliability of an impression is backed up by all the other impressions and notions related to it.

3. Finally, we may be able to act upon chances that not only look worth taking on a fifty-fifty basis and are uncontradicted and backed up by the experiences of other people, but have been thoroughly investigated and found to have solid reasons for taking them. In other words, we may be able to discover a "system" for life's gamble that mathematically, so to speak, ought to work. Then, says Carneades, we have a basis for action that is probable, undisputed, and tested (Fuller, *Philosophy*, pp. 277,278).

Clitomachus (sometimes spelled Cleitomachus) was the third leader. He attacked the three degrees of probability, opting for a more uniform system of Skepticism.

Sensationalistic Skepticism was the last of the classical schools of Skepticism. Its two most prominent leaders were Aenesidemus of Gnossus (first century B.C.) and Sextus Empiricus (200 A.D.). Aenesidemus exposed what he felt were fallacious tests for truth: sensation and confirmed opinion. He felt that these were subjective tests and could not be trusted. However, he had no objective tests for truth and instead was a confirmed skeptic, viewing life and existence as uncertain but livable on the

---

[4]*Stoics*—an Athenian school of philosophy founded around 305 B.C. by Zeno of Citium in Cyprus. *Stoicism*—"For Stoicism virtue alone is the only good and the virtuous man is the one who has attained happiness through knowledge, as Socrates had taught. The virtuous man thus finds happiness in himself and is independent of the external world which he has succeeded in overcoming by mastering himself, his passions and emotions. As for the Stoic conception of the universe as a whole, their doctrine is pantheistic. All things and all natural laws follow by a conscious determination from the basic World-Reason, and it is this rational order by which, according to Stoicism, the wise man seeks to regulate his life as his highest duty" (Runes, *Philosophy*, p. 301).

basis of custom and probability. Sextus Empiricus was a doctor, from the empiricist school of doctors, and he put forth the maxim that life should be ordered by observation, or empiricism. Loyal to skepticism, Sextus promoted the study of Socrates' remark, "All that I know is that I know nothing." Sextus set forth his skepticism as follows:

> The *archē*, or motive, for skepticism was the hope of reaching *ataraxia*, the state of "unperturbedness." ... Sextus Empiricus' skepticism had three stages: antithesis, *epochē* (suspension of judgment), and *ataraxia*. The first stage involved a presentation of contradictory claims about the same subject. These claims were so constructed that they were in opposition to one another, and appeared equally probable or improbable.... The second state is *epochē*, or the suspension of judgment. Instead of either asserting or denying any one claim about the subject at hand, one must embrace all mutually inconsistent claims and withhold judgment on each of them. The final stage is *ataraxia*, a state of unperturbedness, happiness, and peace of mind. When that occurs one is freed from dogmatism. He can live peacefully and undogmatically in the world, following his natural inclinations and the laws or customs of society (Geisler and Feinberg, *Philosophy*, pp. 85, 86).

Skepticism died out for the most part during the ascendency of Christianity. It did not become a noticeable philosophical movement again until the post-Reformation period of western European thought with Bishop John Wilkins (1614-1672) and Joseph Glanvill (1636-1680). They are sometimes called "mitigated skeptics." While clinging tenaciously to one area of skepticism, they compromised by not embracing skepticism as the answer to all knowledge problems in all fields. They distinguished between two types of knowledge. The first type, which they agreed was unreliable, was called "infallibly certain knowledge." Nothing, in other words, could be known infallibly and certainly. However, the second type of knowledge, by which one could order life, was called "indubitably certain knowledge." This was knowledge that one had no reason, experience, evidence, or report by which to doubt its veracity. Using this knowledge, Wilkins and Glanvill developed their own system of determining truth within the limits of "reasonable doubt."

Rene Descartes (1596-1650) wrote at the same time as Wilkins and Glanvill, although he is not considered to be a "mitigated skeptic." As a Christian theist, he used skepticism as a tool to prove the existence of God. Rather than seeing skepticism as an end in itself, he saw it as the way to begin to show the undeniability of the existence of God.

> For Descartes, skepticism was not the conclusion of some argument, but the method whereby all doubt could be overcome. Descartes claimed that it is possible to arrive at indubitable knowledge through the rigorous and systematic application of doubt to one's beliefs (ibid., p. 91).

From the time of Descartes, the majority of such thinkers have been atheists or agnostics. We will treat some of these skeptical thinkers more thoroughly in the historical sections on atheism and agnosticism. However, we will mention them briefly here.

David Hume (1711-1776) is known as a metaphysical[5] skeptic. He believed that it was impossible to have any accurate knowledge about anything metaphysical. He pointed out that standards of probability for beliefs go beyond our immediate experience and must be accepted with some measure of faith.

Nicholas Horvath in his book, *Philosophy*, explains that:

> Hume claimed that only sense-knowledge based on experience is possible. Ideas are mere copies of sense impressions. Impressions and ideas constitute the human intellect. Ideas are not entirely unconnected; there is a bond of union between them and one calls up another. This phenomenon is called association of ideas.
>
> Neither material nor spiritual substances exist in reality; their ideas are purely imaginative concepts, being nothing other than a constant association of impressions. Likewise there is nothing in man's experience that justifies a notion of necessary connection or causation; cause and effect designate merely a regular succession of ideas. Since the principle of causality is mere expectation due to custom, no facts outside consciousness are known to man.
>
> Granted the negation of substance, the existence of God and the immortality of the human soul are only hypothetical. Freedom of will is an illusion; virtue is that which pleases,

[5]In this context, "metaphysical" means that which is unable to be tested by the senses.

> and vice is that which displeases (Nicholas A. Horvath, *Philosophy*, Woodbury, NY: Barron's Educational Series, Inc., 1974, pp. 88,89).

More recently, A. J. Ayer (1910-1970), a limited skeptic, taught that any talk about metaphysics is meaningless. In addition, Albert Camus (1913-1960), one of the most important of all the so-called "irrational" skeptics, asserted that there is no meaning, no knowledge that is objectively true, and no objective value. The entire history of skepticism has the same basic theme. It suspends judgment about truth. At various times skeptics have said that even their statement of skepticism is doubtful. At other times they have said that the one non-skeptical statement is the same statement, that skepticism is doubtful.

Atheism

Although the term *atheism* as a reference to the belief that God (or gods) does (do) not exist dates from the late sixteenth century, Niccolo Machiavelli (d. 1527) had already promoted a social ethic which did not depend on belief in, or the existence of, a supreme God. In his satirical essay, *The Prince*, he taught that the ruler ought to rule wisely and justly in order *to secure his position and to satisfy his ego*, rather than to satisfy some divine mandate. Machiavelli was one of the first to champion the then novel idea that "the end justifies the means." He argued that a ruler should not burden his subjects too much, not because it would be morally wrong to do so, but because it would not be expedient, for his oppressed subjects would then be more likely to revolt, depose him, and perhaps even kill him for his cruelty. Although Machiavelli cannot be termed an actual atheist, his system for successful governorship does not depend on, or presuppose, any divine order to this world.

Ideas from many philosophers, not all of whom were actually atheists, helped shape the atheistic philosophy of today.

During the enlightenment of the eighteenth century, Baron P. H. T. d'Holbach referred to an atheist as

> a man who destroys the dreams and chimerical beings that are dangerous to the human race so that men can be brought back to nature, to experience, and to reason (*Enclyclopaedia*

Britannica, Chicago, et. al.: Encyclopaedia Britannica, Inc., 1978, *Macropaedia*, II, p. 259).

As a brief and circumscribed overview of the history of atheism, we will review some of the contributions to modern atheism made by Hegel, Feuerbach, Marx, Comte, Nietzsche, Jaspers, and Sartre. Ideas from philosophers such as Bayle, Spinoza, Fichte, and Hume, although not mentioned here, also contributed to the development of modern atheistic thought.

Georg W. F. Hegel (1770-1831) was the man whose writings became an inspiration for the modern atheistic movement. He was one of the first prominent philosophers to advance the idea that God[6] was dependent upon the world at least as much as the world was dependent upon God. He said that without the world God is not God. In some way, God needed His creation. This was the first step in saying that, since God was not sufficient in Himself, He was then unnecessary and ultimately imaginary.

Ludwig Feuerbach (1804-1872) was an early prominent atheistic philosopher. He denied all supernaturalism and attributed all talk about God to talk about nature. Man, he said, is dependent not on God, but on nature. Feuerbach promoted what is sometimes referred to as the wish-fulfillment idea of God. He postulated that the idea of God arose as a result of men desiring to have some sort of supernatural Being as an explanation for their own existence and the events they observed around them. This

---

[6]Hegel thought of God as Spirit. His concept of God is described by Vincent Miceli: "But Hegel questioned whether the philosophers or the theologians had succeeded in attaining the real God. He protested that the God of Christian experience was an inadequate, a premature, not-yet-developed God. Hegel set himself the task of completing the good news of the Gospels; he would go beyond Christianity by demonstrating that the only valid God was dialectically evolving Thought or Spirit Which gradually, inevitably attains and reveals Itself in conceptual clarity and complete self-consciousness through the entire scope of cosmic and human history. Hegel set himself the mission of rescuing the God of Christianity from the vagueness of imagery, the symbolism of myths, the simplistic charm of parables" (Vincent P. Miceli, *The Gods of Atheism*, New Rochelle, NY: Arlington House, 1971, pp. 21, 22).

wish, or desire, was the seed from which the God-myth grew. Feuerbach thought this hypothesis proved that God actually did not exist.

Hegel and Feuerbach strongly influenced Karl Marx (1818-1883) and his collaborator, Frederich Engels (1820-1895). Marx, an avowed atheist, preached that religion is the opiate of the people and the enemy of all progress. Part of the task of the great proletariat revolution is the destruction of all religion.

Auguste Comte (1798-1857) was an early contemporary of Marx and Engels. He believed that God was an irrelevant superstition. As a result, Comte divided human development into three main stages:

> "the Theological, or fictitious," "the Metaphysical, or abstract" and the Scientific, or positive." In the first the human mind looks for first causes and "supposes all phenomena to be produced by the immediate action of supernatural beings." The second is a transitional stage where the mind searches for "abstract forces" behind phenomena. But in the third and ultimate stage man's mind applies itself to the scientific study of the laws according to which things work. God and the supernatural are left behind as irrelevant superstition (Colin Brown, *Philosophy and the Christian Faith*, Downers Grove, IL: InterVarsity Press, 1968, pp. 241, 142).

Friedrich Nietzsche (1844-1900) is often called the Father of the Death of God School. He laid the cornerstone for later nihilists by teaching that since God does not exist, man must devise his own way of life.

Karl Jaspers (1883-1969) and Martin Heidegger (1889-1971) were two prominent existentialist thinkers who discussed the ambiguous (and therefore meaningless) nature of religious transcendence. In addition, Heidegger stressed that one's salvation lay in his own independence as an individual separated from every other individual, including, of course, any sort of God.

Jean-Paul Sartre (1905-1981) was the most popular proponent of existentialism. He argued that man not only creates his own destiny, but that each man has only himself as the sole justification for his existence. There is no ultimate, objective, eternal meaning to life. An individual simply exists without reference to others.

A good example of atheistic perspective is contained in the *Humanist Manifesto* (1933). It was composed and signed by leading secular humanists who declared, in part, that "Humanism is faith in the supreme value and self-perfectability of human personality." Although there have been many other important thinkers in the history of atheism, these are representative of the most influential contributors shaping modern atheistic thought. Other modern atheistic thinkers are discussed in some of the references mentioned in the bibliography.

Agnosticism

Although agnosticism is a very broad field, we have chosen to limit our historical discussion of it to three of the most influential philosophers in its recent expressions. As we stated before, there is some overlap among atheism, agnosticism and skepticism, and many of the philosophers important in the development of one are also important to the others.

David Hume (1711-1776), known for promoting metaphysical skepticism, showed the close marriage between skepticism and agnosticism. As a British Empiricist, he declared that the probabilistic standards for beliefs go beyond our immediate experience. We act on faith, then, not on knowledge. We do not know for sure: we are agnostic. However, we still act, having chosen to trust faith while at the same time being prepared for faith to let us down. Belief is not to be confused with ultimate truth, which is unknowable.

Immanuel Kant (1724-1804), although a theist, developed Hume's skepticism into metaphysical agnosticism. He believed it was impossible to know reality and consequently impossible to know metaphysical reality.

Colin Brown credits T. H. Huxley (1825-1895) with the term *agnostic*.

> The word agnosticism is of much more recent coinage. It is generally ascribed to T. H. Huxley, the Victorian scientist and friend of Charles Darwin, who devised it to describe his own state of mind. He used it, not to deny God altogether, but to express doubt as to whether knowledge could be attained, and to protest ignorance on 'a great many things that the -ists and the -ites about me professed to be familiar with' (ibid., p. 132).

Hume, Kant and Huxley represent a short history of contemporary agnosticism, which is distinguished by its assertion that one cannot know. Other prominent agnostics include Charles Darwin and Bertrand Russell.

Arguments Against the Existence of God

We will now summarize five types of arguments most nontheists use against the existence of God, and then give a Christian response to each. Space limitations preclude direct quotes, but some of the most important thinkers on these arguments include Immanuel Kant and Georg Hegel in addition to those we refer to.

It is not important here to distinguish atheism, agnosticism, and skepticsm from each other since non-believers of all three persuasions can use each of the arguments in various forms. But an understanding of these five arguments will give the reader useful principles for responding to many of the arguments against God's existence.

These areas of our divisions (languages, knowledge, moral concepts, scientific methods, and logic) are not strictly demarcated nor are they generally accepted philosophical categorizations, but they are simply made as a convenience to the reader. They will help you find that area of argument in which you are most particularly interested.

Language

EXAMPLE: *Talking about God is meaningless.*

"There are only two kinds of meaningful statements. A statement can be purely definitional (all triangles have three sides) without telling us about the real world (whether triangles actually exist). Or, a statement can be about reality by containing empirically verifiable (testable by the senses) information (this is a triangle). To talk about God in purely definitional statements does not tell us if He actually exists. However, because He is not empirically verifiable, we cannot make empirically verifiable statements about Him. Since purely definitional and empirically verifiable statements are the only kinds of meaningful statements there are, to talk of God's existence is meaningless or [as it is often put] non-sense."

This argument does not actually deny that God exists, but declares all talk about Him futile. Leading thinkers on this subject include A. J. Ayer, Paul van Buren, and Ludwig Wittgenstein.

Knowledge

EXAMPLE: *We can't know the real.*

"We can know about things in the real world through the use of our senses and our mind. However, since our senses are imperfect and selective, and our mind is affected by all it has experienced previously, our perception of a thing is thereby affected. Therefore, we can know a thing as it is to us,* but not as it is in itself."**

This does not argue specifically against God's existence, but can be used to deny that one can know objectively about God. Immanuel Kant and David Hume were instrumental in developing this theory of knowledge.

Moral Concepts

EXAMPLE: *The Christian God could not allow evil.*

"If there were an all-powerful God, then He could destroy all evil. If He were all-good, then He would want to destoy all evil. If your all-powerful, all-good God existed, then He would have had to destroy all evil. Evil exists. Therefore, your all-powerful, all-good God must not exist. Or, if He exists, He is not able to do away with evil."

This idea does not argue against the existence of all gods, but only against this "all-powerful, all-good God." From this basis the other problems of evil emerge. Among those issues are the suffering of innocents, natural calamities, etc. One of the earliest proponents of this idea was Epicurus. More modern thinkers were David Hume and J. L. Mackie.

Scientific Methods

EXAMPLE 1: *God is man's wish (Psychology).*

"Man feels inadequate in himself. He wishes for Someone who is big enough to rescue him from life's

---

* Kant termed this the "phenomenal world."

** Kant termed this the "noumenal world."

tragedies. He desires God to exist. God arises from man's mind. Therefore, God has no objective reality. He does not exist."

Leading supporters of this idea included Ludwig Feuerbach, Friedrich Nietzsche, and Sigmund Freud.

EXAMPLE 2: *God is a result of superstitious belief (Sociology).*

"Primitive man could not explain the world around him in natural terms. He invented God to explain the unknown. Today science has shown us the natural laws governing our world. Natural laws explain everything. We no longer need belief in God to explain things. Therefore, God does not exist."

Some of those instrumental in developing this argument included David Hume, Sir James George Frazer, Sir Edward Burnett Tylor, and Bertrand Russell.

Logic

Example 1: *God's all-powerfulness is contradictory.*

"There cannot be an omnipotent (all-powerful) God. Such a God would be stuck with the following contradictory questions (antimonies):

1. Can God create a rock too heavy for Him to lift?
2. Can God make 2 + 2 = 6?
3. Can God make Himself go out of existence and then pop back into existence?
4. Can God make a square circle?

If God is all-powerful, He should be able to do these things. But, in doing them, He is thwarting His own omnipotence. He must not exist."

EXAMPLE 2: *God's attributes contradict each other.*

"How can one being possess both love and wrath? How can God be all-loving (giving man free will) but be all-knowing (predestining man's actions by His foreknowledge)? How can God be absolutely good and yet absolutely free (able to choose evil)? Because God's attributes contradict each other logically, He must not exist."

Christian Responses

Encountering a variety of arguments against the existence of God at one time can be overwhelming. Many Christian students who are unfamiliar with secular philosophy sometimes are at a loss to answer those arguments when they are first confronted with them. We have presented a few of the most common arguments which are representative of the skeptical/agnostic/atheistic attitude prevalent in many secular circles today. (For further discussion of such arguments, see the books referred to in the Bibliography.) We have found that most arguments against the existence of God can be answered by the simple principles we will present below. Due to space limitations the arguments and our responses have been simplified. However, we are confident that the reader can establish a reasonable defense against such arguments with the following principles and personal study.

Refutation of Skepticism

Skepticism is a powerful tool in the hands of an agnostic or atheist. As we saw in our definition and history sections, skepticism is utilized in many areas of non-theistic thought. It often is presupposed or asserted openly as part of an argument against the existence of God. For this reason, we shall deal with the claims of skepticism before we deal with the specific arguments raised above.

Skepticism is ultimately meaningless. It refutes itself. If one declares, "You can never be sure about anything," he is catching himself in his own trap. If we can be sure of nothing, then we cannot be sure of the statement, "nothing is certain." But, if that statement is objectively true, then we can be sure about one thing, the statement. But, if we can be sure about the statement, then the statement must be false. If the statement is false, then we cannot be sure. The inexorable fate of the skeptic is to be condemned by his own sentence.

The Sahakians comment:

> Nihilism and Skepticism are both self-contradictory and self-defeating philosophies. If truth does not exist (Nihilism), then the posited truth of Nihilism could not exist. If knowledge is impossible (Skepticism), how could we ever come to know that? Apparently some things can be known.
>
> Even the less extreme view of Protagoras is self-defeating, as demonstrated by Plato's charming argument in the following paragraphs....
>
> PROTAGORAS: Truth is relative, it is only a matter of opinion.

> SOCRATES: You mean that truth is mere subjective opinion?
> PROTAGORAS: Exactly. What is true for you is true for you, and what is true for me, is true for me. Truth is subjective.
> SOCRATES: Do you really mean that? That my opinion is true by virtue of its being my opinion?
> PROTAGORAS: Indeed I do.
> SOCRATES: My opinion is: Truth is absolute, not opinion, and that you, Mr. Protagoras, are absolutely in error. Since this is my opinion, then you must grant that it is true according to your philosophy.
> PROTAGORAS: You are quite correct, Socrates. (Sahakian and Sahakian, *Ideas*, p. 28).

Geisler and Feinberrg continue in the same vein:

> . . . The skeptic's assertion that we cannot know anything is itself a claim about knowledge. If the skeptic's claim is false, then we need not worry about the skeptic's charge. On the other hand, if it is true, then his position is self-contradictory, because we know at least one thing—that we cannot know anything.
> . . . But suppose that the skeptic responds by saying that we have misunderstood his claim. He is not claiming that the sentence, "You cannot know anything" is either true or false. . . . The skeptic's position is shown to be necessarily false, for his is still a claim about knowledge: "For all sentences, we know that we cannot know whether they are true or false." Therefore, total or complete skepticism is rationally inconsistent (Geisler and Feinberg, *Philosophy*, p. 94).

Christians who often encounter non-believers (agnostics or atheists) find that many arguments against the existence of God or the claims of Christianity are basically claims that one cannot know. They are essentially skeptical arguments and are self-refuting. This one principle is sufficient for answering several anti-theistic arguments.

Refutation of Language Argument

The language argument is self-refuting, just as skepticism is self-refuting. To say that one cannot talk meaningfully about God is to talk meaningfully about God. Either one's statement ("One cannot talk meaningfully about God") is meaningful, in which case it gives us meaningful information about God, or it is, itself, meaningless, in which case we need not heed it. As Geisler puts it,

> . . . the principles of empirical verifiability as set forth by Ayer is self-defeating. For it is neither purely definitional nor strictly factual. Hence, on its own grounds it would fall into the third category of non-sense statements. . . . the attempt to limit meaning to the definitional or to the verifiable is to make a truth claim that must itself be subject to some test. If it cannot be tested, then it becomes an unfalsifiable view (Norman Geisler, *Christian Apologetics*, Grand Rapids, MI: Baker Book House, 1976, p. 23).

Refutation of Knowledge Argument

One who adheres completely to the idea that we cannot know the real is another example of one who refutes himself. Reasonably we could say that we do not know *everything* about the real, but it is self-defeating to say one knows *nothing* about the real. If one really knows nothing about the real, then his statement ("I know nothing about the real") is false: he really knows the truth of his statement. His statement cannot be true unless, contradictorily, it is also false. The Christian philosopher Warren Young put it this way:

> The basis of the possibility of knowing rests on a belief in the rationality of the human mind. Apart from belief in rationality, knowledge is impossible. Unless the organizing ability of the mind be granted, it is impossible to know. The data organized by reason are the data of human experience. In spite of the skeptic's rejection of the reliability of experience, his answer is not final. Man is not only deceived by his senses, but in almost all cases he *knows* that he is being deceived. His reason leads him to compensate for possible deception, to interpret sense data properly, and so he is able to know (Young, *Philosophy*, p. 62).

Geisler also discusses this dilemma with his analysis of complete agnosticism. He writes,

> Complete agnosticism is self-defeating; it reduces to the self-destructing assertion that "one knows enough about reality in order to affirm that nothing can be known about reality." This statement provides within itself all that is necessary to falsify itself. For if one knows *something* about reality, then he surely cannot affirm in the same breath that *all* of reality is unknowable. And of course if one knows nothing whatsoever about reality, then he has no basis whatsoever for making a

statement about reality. It will not suffice to say that his knowledge about reality is purely and completely negative, that is, a knowledge of what one cannot meaningfully affirm that something is *not*—that it follows that total agnosticism is self-defeating because it assumes some knowledge about reality in order to deny any knowledge of reality (Geisler, *Apologetics*, p. 20).

Refutation of Moral Concepts Argument

The argument of the problem of evil and its various forms and development is probably the most frequently used argument against the existence of God. Whole books are devoted to a Christian reconciliation of the problem. Whole books are devoted to exploring the ideas of non-Christian proponents of the concept. Many sub-arguments against God's existence come from this basic argument. Why does God allow babies to suffer and die? Why are there innocent murder victims? Why does God allow natural calamities?, etc. By understanding the basic problems with the view, one can learn the principles for answering the different forms the view takes.

A good way to find answers to such arguments is to look at each step of the argument and see whether or not it tells the truth. If even one step of the argument is invalid or untrue, then the weight of the entire argument crashes down. When we examine this argument, we find little disagreement with its first step (premise): "If there were an all-powerful God, He could destroy all evil." We begin to have problems with the second premise: "If He were all-good, He would want to destroy all evil." There are two problems here. First, an all-good God may have beneficent uses for evil. Second, the arguer has not taken into consideration the element of time. What if God were to use evil for a time and *then*, ultimately, destroy it? That would allow for a good God and yet also allow evil at this present time.

Richard Purtill sums it up this way:

> Now on this view there can be a problem of evil, since some things that happen in the world seem to be contrary to what a loving God would permit. But the problem must somehow be soluble, since the events we condemn and the moral law by which we condemn them are both traceable to the same Source. If God is what Christianity says he is, he is the God of Love and Justice, and also the God who permits apparently

> useless suffering. It must be, then, that there is a reconciliation. (Perhaps the suffering is *not* useless, for example.) Thus evil is a problem for Christianity, but not an objection to it. The view that admits a problem holds out the hope of a solution (Purtill, *Reason*, p. 52).

Geisler and Feinberg point out some of the problems:

> The theist responds by first pointing out that (the) premise... places an unjustified time limit on God. It says, in effect, that since God has not yet done anything to defeat evil we are absolutely sure He never will. But this cannot be known for certain by any finite mind. It is possible that God will yet defeat evil in the future. This is indeed what Christians believe, for it is predicted in the Bible (Revelation 20-22) (Geisler and Feinberg, *Philosophy*, pp. 274, 275).

Refutation of Scientific Methods Arguments

To say that man's wish for God to exist proves that God does *not* exist is completely illogical. Because I wish for my children to grow up as strong Christians is no proof that they will grow up as atheists. My wishing does not make things exist, nor does it preclude things from existing. The arguments for the existence of God must be taken on their own merits, regardless of whether men have wished for God to exist. Does the fact that atheists wish for God *not* to exist prove that He *does* exist? Of course not. One must look at the evidence.

In the same manner, the idea that man (or at least some men) derived their belief in God from superstition says nothing about whether or not that God actually exists. In *Ideas of the Great Philosophers*, this is identified as the genetic fallacy in logic:

> ...According to this argument, religion was spawned in fear, superstition, and ignorance; and fear of the unknown, at a time of ignorance concerning scientific causes, drove man to superstition.
>
> Logicians criticize the preceding argument as an example of a *genetic fallacy*, the error of assuming that a point has been proved merely because it has been traced to its source. It may be of interest, and definitely is of interest to at least the psychologist and the historian, to ascertain how our religious beliefs emerged and what gave them their initial impetus, but so far as proof of Atheism is concerned, such factors are irrelevant. Thus, evidence that a particular science grew out

of magic or alchemy does not imply that science today is invalid (Sahakian and Sahakian, *Ideas*, p. 102).

Richard Purtill quickly took apart the argument when he wrote:

> Let us begin with the accusation that Christianity represents a pre-scientific, "magical" view of the world. Of course Christianity is pre-scientific in the sense that it began before modern science began. So, for that matter, did mathematics, logic, history, and a great many other things. But that Christianity is *opposed* to a genuinely scientific view of the universe we will deny. As for the accusation that Christianity represents a "magical" view of the universe, "magical" here either just means un- or antiscientific, or else it has some connection with historical beliefs in magic. This is a confusion. Magic, as believed in for many centuries, was an attempt to exert power over nature by means of words, ceremonies, mixtures of materials, etc. It was essentially an attempt of a sort of technology, an attempt to master forces that would give men power, wealth, and secret knowledge. Insofar as it was an attempt to satisfy curiosity and give power over nature, it was the ancestor of science rather than of religion.
>
> Christianity, on the other hand, believes that certain wonderful events have occurred, sometimes as an answer to prayer. But these events are the result of the will of the Person who created nature and its laws, and could not be predicted, demanded, or forced. The effects of these events may sometimes be beneficial to men but their purpose is to reveal something about God or to authenticate such a revelation. The whole attitude and atmosphere of magic and Christianity are opposed. On the one hand you have the magician, with his secret knowledge, forcing certain things to occur by his spells or potions. On the other hand you have the Christian saint with his message for all men, praying that God's will be done, and sometimes finding a marvelous response to his prayer. The two things are poles apart (Purtill, *Reason*, pp. 38,39).

Refutation of Logic Arguments

Arguments which attempt to make the Christian God self-contradictory are many. However, almost all of them concern God's attributes. The most popular target is God's omnipostence or all-powerfulness. We listed just a few of the arguments that supposedly argue against the omnipotence of God. What does it mean when we can say that God is all-powerful? Do we mean that he can do anything we can imagine?

No. When we say that God is all-powerful, we mean that anything which is capable of being done, God can do. He cannot do the logically or intrinsically impossible. The Christian theologian James Oliver Buswell, Jr. writes,

> . . . omnipotence does not mean that God can do anything, but it does mean that He can do with power anything that power can do. He has all the power that is or could be.
>
> Can God make two plus two equal six? This is a question which is frequently asked by skeptics and by children. We reply by asking how much power it would take to bring about this result. The absurdity of the question is not too difficult to see. Would the power of a ton of dynamite make two plus two equal six? or the power of an atom bomb? or of a hydrogen bomb? When these questions are asked it is readily seen that the truth of the multiplication tables is not in the realm of power. Power has nothing to do with it. When we assert that God is omnipotent, we are talking about power (James Oliver Buswell, Jr., *A Systematic Theology of the Christian Religion*, Grand Rapids, MI: Zondervan Publishing House, 1962, pp. 63,64).

Sahakian and Sahakian point out that this sort of logical argument is logically inconsistent. It is known as the fallacy of contradictory premises.

> . . . When contradictory premises are present in an argument, one premise cancels out the other. It is possible for one or the other of the two premises to be true, but not for both to be simultaneously true. Note the contradictory premises in the following questions: "If God is all-powerful, can he put himself out of existence, then come to life with twice the power he had originally?" "Can God make a stone so heavy that he cannot lift it?" "Can God make a round square?" "What would happen if an irrestible force met an immovable object?" (One student's answer: "An inconceivable smash!") (Sahakian and Sahakian, *Ideas*, p. 23).

The principle is spelled out clearly in Thomas Warren's words:

> Rather than saying that God *cannot* do the things just referred to, it would be more in harmony with the truth to say simply that such things *cannot be done at all!* God is infinite in power, but power meaningfully relates only to that which *can* be done, to what is *possible* of accomplishment—

not to what is *impossible*! It is absurd to speak of any power (even infinite power) being able (having the power) to do what simply *cannot* be done. God *can* do whatever is *possible* to be done, but he *will* do only what is in harmony with *his* nature. Rather than saying that God *cannot* make a four-sided triangle, one would more accurately (or, perhaps, more meaningfully) say (in the light of the fact that the word "triangle" means a *three*-sided figure and cannot refer to any *four*-sided figure) that the making of four-sided triangles simply cannot be done (Thomas B. Warren, *Have Atheists Proved There is No God?*, Nashville, TN: Gospel Advocate Company, 1972, pp. 27,28).

With the preceding thorough refutation of the problems with God's omnipotence, it seems hardly worthwhile to examine the other claims to God's self-contradictions. However, a quick look will show that such purported contradictions are not contradictions at all. The Christian God has a unified nature of complementary attributes. None cancel out any others.

If we simply examine the presuppositions of the arguments, we can see their problems. For example, the skeptic is presupposing that God's love and His wrath (the pouring-out of His justice) are mutually exclusive. We would answer by bringing it to a human level. No one would argue that a father's discipline of his child or a judge's punishment of a criminal proves that the father or judge have no love. On the contrary, their justice should work with their love.

While we would agree that it is loving for God to give man free will, we would not agree that foreknowledge causes predestination. Merely knowing the future does not predetermine it. Finally, freedom for the infinitely good and eternal (never changing) God does not have to include the ability to choose evil to be genuine freedom. Freedom does not mean freedom to contradict one's nature. God's nature is immutably good, holy, and perfect. (By perfect we mean complete.) His will is the self-expression of his nature and as such His will is necessarily good, holy, and perfect.

Geisler sums up the unity of God's attributes in the following way:

Perfections such as love and justice are not incompatible in God. They are different, but not everything different is incompatible. What is different, and sometimes at least seemingly incompatible in this world, is not necessarily incompatible in God. For example, there can be such a thing as just-love or loving-justice. Likewise, God can be all-knowing and all-loving, for his infinite knowledge may be exercised in allowing men the freedom to do evil without coercing them (in accordance with his love) against their will so that through it all he may achieve (by infinite power) the greatest good for all (in accordance with his justice) (Geisler, *Apologetics*, p. 229).

Conclusion

While we have just touched the surface of the broad fields of atheism, agnosticism, and skepticism, we have tried to give viable Christian responses to some of the most significant arguments against the existence of God. We urge the reader to check the bibliography for more intensive study of the subject.

As Christians in a non-Christian world we alternately defend the gospel (1 Peter 3:15) and aggressively proclaim the truth (Acts 2:14-39). God is no stranger to logic and philosophy. His Word will endure long after the thoughts of men have turned to ashes (1 Peter 1:25).

The apostle Paul was not afraid to preach Jesus Christ among the non-believing philosophers of his day. He proclaimed to them:

> For while I was passing through and examining the objects of your worship, I also found an altar with this inscription, "TO AN UNKNOWN GOD." What therefore you worship in ignorance, this I proclaim to you.
>
> The God who made the world and all things in it, since He is Lord of heaven and earth, does not dwell in temples made with hands; neither is He served by human hands, as though He needed anything, since He Himself gives to all life and breath and all things... that they should seek God, if perhaps they might grope for Him, though He is not far from each one of us (Acts 17:23-25,27 NASB).

Atheism Extended Bibliography

Note: The bibliography is divided into three parts. The first part lists general references. The second part lists books and authors from a generally nontheistic position. The third part lists books and authors which can be used to support a general theistic position. Not all of the authors listed in this third section are evangelical Christians.

General Reference

Angeles, Peter, *Dictionary of Philosophy.* NY: Harper and Row, Publishers, 1981.

Avey, Albert E., *Handbook in the History of Philosophy.* NY: Harper and Row, Publishers, 1954.

Frost, S. E., Jr., *Basic Teachings of the Great Philosophers.* Garden City, NY: Doubleday and Company, Inc., 1942, 1962.

Fuller, B. A. G., *A History of Philosophy.* NY: Holt, Rinehart and Winston, 1955.

Hook, Sidney, ed., *Philosophy and History: A Symposium.* NY: New York University Press, 1963.

Horvath, Nicholas A. *Philosophy.* Woodbury, NY: Barron's Educational Series, Inc., 1974.

Joad, C. E. M., *Guide to Philosophy.* London: Victor Gollancz, Ltd., 1955.

Runes, Dagobert D., ed., *Dictionary of Philosophy.* Totowa, NJ: Littlefield, Adams and Company, 1960, 1962.

Sahakian, William, *History of Philosophy.* NY: Harper and Row, Publishers, 1968.

Sahakian, William and Mabel, *Ideas of the Great Philosophers.* NY: Harper and Row, Publishers, 1966.

Nontheistic

Ayer, A. J., *Language, Truth, and Logic.* NY: Dover Publications, 1946.

Dewey, John, *A Common Faith.* New Haven, CT: Yale University Press, 1934.

Feuerbach, Ludwig, *The Essence of Christianity.* NY: Harper and Row, Publishers, 1957.

Flew, Antony, *God and Philosophy.* NY: Dell Books, 1966.

Freud, Sigmund, *The Future of an Illusion.* NY: Doubleday and Company, 1927.

Kaufmann, Walter, *Critique of Religion and Philosophy.* NY: Harper and Row, Publishers, 1958.

____________, ed., *The Portable Nietzsche.* NY: The Viking Press, 1954.

Madden, Edward H., and Peter H. Hare, *Evil and the Concept of God.* Springfield, IL: Charles C. Thomas, Publishers, 1968.

Marx, Karl, and Friedrich Engels, *On Religion.* NY: Schocken Books, 1964.

Matson, Wallace I., *The Existence of God.* Ithaca, NY: Cornell University Press, 1965.

Nielson, Kai, *Contemporary Critiques of Religion.* NY: Seabury Press, 1972.

____________, *Ethics without God.* Buffalo, NY: Prometheus Books, 1973.

____________, *Skepticism.* NY: St. Martin's Press, 1973.

Russell, Bertrand, *Religion and Science.* NY: Oxford University Press, 1935.

____________, *Why I Am Not a Christian.* NY: Simon and Schuster, 1957.

Sartre, Jean-Paul, *Existentialism and Human Emotions.* NY: Philosophical Library, 1957.

Theistic

Adler, Mortimer J., *How to Think About God: A Guide for the 20th-Century Pagan.* NY: Macmillan Publishing Company, Inc., 1980.

Baillie, John, *Our Knowledge of God.* NY: Charles Scribner's Sons, 1959.

Benignus, Brother, *Nature, Knowledge and God: An Introduction to Thomistic Philosophy.* Milwaukee, WI: The Bruce Publishing Company, 1947.

Bowne, Borden P., *Theism.* NY: American Book Company, 1887, 1902.

Brown, Colin, *Philosophy and the Christian Faith.* Downers Grove, IL: InterVarsity Press, 1968.

Buswell, James Oliver, Jr., *A Systematic Theology of the Christian Religion.* Grand Rapids, MI: Zondervan Publishing House, 1962.

Carnell, Edward J., *A Philosophy of the Christian Religion.* Grand Rapids, MI: William B. Eerdmans Publishing Company, 1952.

Custance, Arthur C., *Evolution or Creation?* Grand Rapids, MI: Zondervan Publishing House, 1976.

Fairbairn, A. M., *The Philosophy of the Christian Religion.* NY: Macmillan Publishing Company, Inc., 1903.

Fitch, William, *God and Evil: Studies in the Mystery of Suffering and Pain.* Grand Rapids, MI: William B. Eerdmans Publishing Company, 1967.

Flint, Robert, *Agnosticism.* NY: Charles Scribner's Sons, 1903.

____________, *Anti-Theistic Theories.* London: William Blackwood and Sons, 1899.

Geisler, Norman, *Christian Apologetics.* Grand Rapids, MI: Baker Book House, 1976.

____________, *Philosophy of Religion.* Grand Rapids, MI: Zondervan Publishing House, 1974.

____________, and Paul Feinberg, *Introduction to Philosophy: A Christian Perspective.* Grand Rapids, MI: Baker Book House, 1980.

Gerstner, John, *Reasons for Faith.* NY: Harper and Row, Publishers, 1960.

Gore, Charles, *The Reconstruction of Belief.* London: John Murray, 1926.

Hackett, Stuart, *The Resurrection of Theism.* Chicago, IL: Moody Press, 1957.

Hick, John, *Arguments for the Existence of God.* NY: Herder and Herder, 1971.

Jay, Eric G., *The Existence of God.* London: Society for Promoting Christian Knowledge, 1946.

Lewis, C. S., *Mere Christianity.* NY: Macmillan Publishing Company, Inc., 1952.

____________, *Miracles.* NY: Macmillan Publishing Company, Inc., 1947, 1960.

____________, *The Problem of Pain.* NY: Macmillan Publishing Company, Inc., 1943.

Mascall, E. L., *Existence and Analogy.* London: Longmans, Green and Company, Ltd., 1949.

____________, *The Openness of Being: Natural Theology Today.* Philadelphia, PA: The Westminster Press, 1971.

____________, *Words and Images.* NY: The Ronald Press Company, 1957.

Mavrodes, George I., *Belief in God: A Study in the Epistemology of Religion.* NY: Random House, 1970.

Miceli, Vincent P., *The Gods of Atheism.* New Rochelle, NY: Arlington House, 1971.

Plantinga, Alvin, *God, Freedom, and Evil.* NY: Harper and Row, Publishers, 1974.

Purtill, Richard, *Reason to Believe.* Grand Rapids, MI: William B. Eerdmans Publishing Company, 1974.

Ross, James F., *Philosophical Theology.* NY: Bobbs-Merrill, 1969.

____________, *Introduction to the Philosophy of Religion.* NY: Macmillan Publishing Company, Inc., 1972.

Schwarz, Hans, *The Search for God.* Minneapolis, MN: Augsburg Publishing House, 1975.

Sillen, Edward, *Ways of Thinking About God.* NY: Sheed and Ward, 1961.

Taylor, Richard, *Metaphysics.* Englewood Cliffs, NJ: Prentice Hall, 1974.

Warren, Thomas B., *Have Atheists Proved There is No God?* Nashville, TN: Gospel Advocate Company, 1972.

Young, Warren, *A Christian Approach to Philosophy.* Grand Rapids, MI: Baker Book House, 1954.

CHAPTER TWO

Marxism

Marxism, and its descendant, modern communism, presents a strong challenge to Christianity. Marxism in its various expressions rules a greater number of people in today's world than any other single system. What Vincent P. Miceli observed in 1971 about Marxism is still true today, and now many more are victims of Marxist rule:

> Indeed, today more than one billion persons are ruled by governments that openly profess and practice the doctrine of Marx. And millions of other persons are ruled by governments that fearfully sway to the winds of communist policies. In an age of unprecedented and proliferating crises, there is scarcely a turmoil anywhere in the world in which the catalyzing power of communism may not be discovered. Atheistic communism is a sword of division; it cuts asunder families, communities, nations, empires. It has, indeed, succeeded, directly or indirectly, by action or example, in keeping the world in a state of military conflict since its seizure of power in 1917 (Vincent P. Miceli, *The Gods of Atheism*, New Rochele, NY: Arlington House, 1971, pp. 92, 93).

Marxism is not just politics and economics. Marxism is also a world view, a way of looking at and *explaining* the world. As such, it encompasses philosophy and religion, while paradoxically and vigorously asserting its atheism and contempt for philosophy. The *Encyclopaedia Britannica* points out this quasi-religious nature of Marxism:

> Marxism, which provides remarkable evidence of the power of dominant key ideas to inspire and direct man, is undoubtedly

> one of the greatest challenges to traditional religious belief. . . the thinking of Marx had religious overtones, whether from his own Jewish background or from a Christian atmosphere, not least in Britain where he lived from 1849 to 1883. Second, Marxism can be called a quasi-religion insofar as it calls from its followers a devotion and a commitment that in their empirical character greatly resemble commitment and devotion that characterize religious people. Marxism has undoubtedly fired the spirit of man and given to revolutions, whether in Russia or China, a powerful direction that has maintained stability and avoided anarchy. Furthermore, like a religion, it has provided themes of fulfillment and hope—a revolution interpreted as the initiation of a Communist world society that would be a final consummation. There are many logical similarities between the doctrine of the Marxist millenium and the Christian doctrine of Christ's Second Coming (*Encyclopaedia Britannica III, Macropaedia,* "Philosophy of Religion," Chicago, IL: William Benton, Publisher, 1978, vol. 15, p. 598).

It is the job of philosophy and religion to answer the "why" questions about existence, to give explanations rather than only observing phenomena. While Marx often strongly stressed that his system was *scientific*, and not *philosophical*, he could not excape the realm of philosophy. Because the world view of Marxism attacks the world view of Christianity, we are here addressing that challenge.

In this chapter we will review Karl Marx, the man and his life; briefly discuss thinkers before him who had the most profound effect upon him; and examine those parts of his system which are at root philosophical and atheistic. We will face the atheistic challenge of Marxism in its major manifestations today. Also we will review briefly Marxism's political and economic impact and will see the cohesive Christian world view as presented in the Bible. We will not attempt to present a systematic discussion of Marx's entire system: it has taken others whole volumes to attempt such a task. We shall focus on the core of the system which categorically denies the Christian world view.

Christians cannot remain silent about or, worse, embrace Marxism:

> Marxism and its offspring, Russian Communism, have always maintained world domination as one of their goals. Believing as they do in the inevitability of world revolution and believing that this revolution must be aided and abetted by violence, it is against the very nature of the system for Communists to

"live and let live." It is this aspect of domination which poses a grave threat to the world, especially that part of the world that treasures its traditions and inheritance of democratic, constitutional government. The very existence of the church is sharply challenged....

For Christianity, the conflict becomes most basically a spiritual conflict. In Christianity, Christ becomes the motivating force of all action and is the center of the culture of believers. Marxism and its proponents—though usually referred to as atheistic—have set up their own guiding force which is history itself. This becomes their god, and the motivation for all activity around this is materialistic. Thus they deny God and Christ and spiritual power in history and culture (Thomas O. Kay, *The Christian Answer to Communism*, Grand Rapids, MI: Zondervan Publishing House, 1961, pp. 11, 12).

Karl Marx

The name of Karl Marx is probably the best known name of any founder of a political or economic system. While he made little difference in the societies in which he lived, his system of thought has, in the last hundred years, exerted tremendous influence on the governments and economies of hundreds of countries. The two largest nations in the world, Russia and China, claim him as their ideological father. His ideas have flourished for years, showing a greater strength and stability than the man himself, who spent most of his life in poor health, precarious psychological balance and financial insecurity.

Karl Marx was born in Trier, an ancient German city in the Rhineland (sometimes claimed by France, and known as Treveri). His ancestors, Jewish on both his mother's and father's sides, were rabbis. His father, Heinrich, had converted to Protestantism in 1816 or 1817 in order to continue practicing law after the Prussian edict denying Jews to the bar. Karl was born in 1818 and baptized in 1824, but his mother, Henriette, did not convert until 1825, when Karl was 7. While the family did not appear religious at all—it was said that not a single volume on religion or theology was in Heinrich's modest library—Karl was raised in an atmosphere of religious toleration. There was some discrimination against Jews in the area, but general religious tolerance was the standard. Karl was sent to religious school primarily for academic rather than religious training. On the whole, the family was not committed to either evangelical Protestantism or evangelical Judaism. Vincent Miceli notes:

> The family lived as very liberal Protestants, that is, without any profound religious beliefs. Thus, Karl grew up without an inhibiting consciousness of himself as being Jewish. In changing his credal *allegience*, or course, the father, newly baptized Heinrich, experienced the alienation of turning his back on his religious family and traditions. Thus, though politically emancipated and socially liberated from the ghetto, the experience of being uprooted and not completely at home in the Germany of the nineteenth century did affect the Marx family (Miceli, *Atheism*, pp. 94, 95).

Marx attended the gymnasium (high school) from 1830-1835 and then attended Bonn University (1835-1836). He worked on his doctorate at Berlin University (1836-1841). During this time he met and associated with the Young Hegelians (see below our discussion of Hegel's contributions to Marx's thinking) and suffered a nervous breakdown (1837). His doctoral dissertation was in philosophy and was titled *The Difference between Democritean and Epicurean Philosophy of Nature.* It was accepted by Jena University. His father died in 1838.

Marx's professed atheism and his radical views may have made it difficult for him to be hired as a professor at Prussian-dominated schools and his attention turned to political involvement. His life pattern of revolutionary involvement and intense political activism began to emerge. In 1842 he became the editor of the *Reinische Zeitung,* which was said to be a business periodical. However, this publication had strong radical political views. Marx's philosophy of dialectical materialism and class struggle was already being developed, and often appeared in the pages of the *Reinische Zeitung.*

The year 1843 was an important one for young Marx (25 years old). He met for the first time with Frederich Engels, who was to become his closest friend, benefactor, collaborator, and philosophical and political "soul-mate." He also married Jenny von Westphalen, a baroness to whom he was devoted (in spirit if not always in deed) for the rest of his life. During that same year he wrote two of his early works and they typify his thinking at the time: the "Critique of Hegel's Philosophy of Law," and "On the Jewish Question."

(It is debated whether Marx was specifically anti-semitic or only anti-semitic in the sense that his economic theories had no room for Jewish free enterprise and his presupposed atheism had no room for Jewish religion. Space precludes our discussion of the different sides of this matter. Further discussion can be found in the books listed in the bibliography. Our showing his basic atheistic presuppositions later in this chapter indicate that he at least did reject Judaism.)

That same year also saw the demise of the *Reinische Zeitung*—it became a victim of Prussian censorship—and the expulsion of Marx and his bride from Germany. They moved to Paris in October of 1843.

Carrying his political zeal with him, Marx published the *Deutsche Französische Jahrbücher* in Paris in 1844. This fiery publication earned him expulsion from France, and he moved to Brussels in January-February of 1845.

Marx jumped enthusiastically into the communist activity of Brussels. In 1847 he wrote for the *Deutsche-Brüssler-Zeitung* and organized the *German Communist League* and *German Worker's Association*. At the request of the Brussels communists, Marx and Engels wrote their famous *Communist Manifesto* in 1848. It has become the creed and catechism of Marxist Communism.

Early in 1848 Marx and Jenny were expelled from Brussels, spent a short time in Paris, and returned to Germany as revolutionaries in April. Throwing his entire energies into the workers' fight against the repressive Prussian government, Marx began to publish the *Neue Reinische Zeitung* in June. Less than a year later he was again expelled from Prussia, spent a month in Paris, was expelled from there and moved himself and his family to London (August 24, 1849). For nearly 30 years Marx called London his home. It was there, where he had much more literary freedom than in any country before, that he wrote his monumental work *Das Kapital* which criticized, among other things, British capitalism.

Most of the time they were in London, his family was wretchedly poor. Three of his children died, their illnesses complicated by inadequate shelter, food, and medicine. Although he loved his wife and children devotedly, it was unequal to the passion he felt for his political writing and involvement. Stumpf records:

> While his poverty was deeply humiliating, he was driven with

such single-mindedness to produce his massive books that he could not deviate from this objective to provide his family with more adequate facilities. In addition to his poverty, he was afflicted with a liver ailment and, as Job, was plagued with boils. In this environment his six-year-old son died and his beautiful wife's health failed (Samuel Enoch Stumpf, *Socrates to Sartre: A History of Philosophy*, New York: McGraw-Hill Book Company, 1966, p. 425).

Marx and his wife made many trips to friends and relatives to beg and borrow enough money to pay their debts, feed their children, and finance Marx's political activities. He recognized the sad position in which he put his family, but seemed unable to turn from his profitless writing and organizing to work at any physical labor or occupation that could have provided better for his family. In later years he looked back with regret on the hardships he had made his family endure, commenting:

> You know that I have sacrificed my whole fortune to the revolutionary struggle. I do not regret it. Quite the contrary. If I had to start my life over again, I would do the same. But I would not marry (Saul K. Padover, *Karl Marx: An Intimate Biography* (abridged edition), New York: New American Library, 1978, 1980, p. 280).

In 1851 his illegitimate son, Frederick Demuth, was born to his wife's maid. His wife and children were not told that Frederick was Karl's son. Instead, benefactor, confidant and collaborator Engels was appointed the boy's "father." Not until after her parents' death did Karl's daughter, Eleanor ("Tussy"), learn the truth from Engels.

The years 1849-1853 were times of desperate financial straits for the family but a time when Marx rose to the top of the exiled German communist movement. A personal description of him by a Prussian spy recorded in 1853 reveals the two tensions, poverty and politics, in the Marx household.

> In private life he is a highly disorderly, cynical person, a poor host; he leads a gypsy existence. Washing, grooming, and changing underwear are rarities with him; he gets drunk readily. Often he loafs all day long, but if he has work to do, he works day and night tirelessly. He does not have a fixed time for sleeping and staying up; very often he stays up all night, and at noon he lies down on the sofa fully dressed and sleeps until evening, unconcerned about the comings and goings around him . . .

> Marx lives in one of the worst, and thus cheapest, quarters in London. He lives in two rooms, the one with a view on the street is the living room, the one in the back is the bedroom. In the whole lodging not a single piece of good furniture is to be found; everything is broken, ragged and tattered; everything is covered with fingerthick dust; everywhere the greatest disorder. In the middle of the living room there is a big old table covered with oilcloth. On it lie manuscripts, books, newspapers, the childrens' toys, the scraps of his wife's sewing, tea cups with broken rims, dirty spoons, knives, forks, candlesticks, inkwell, drinking glasses, Dutch clay pipes, tobacco ashes—in a word, everything piled up helter-skelter on the same table. . . (ibid, pp. 155-157).

As destitute as the family was, Karl and Jenny did not neglect the education of their daughters (no legitimate son lived to adulthood), paying for their education in the classics, language, music, art, business, and social graces. While they lived like Marx's beloved proletariat, their daughters were groomed to join the hated bourgeois.

While exiled from Germany, Marx resumed publication of the *Neue Reinische Zeitung.* He wrote it in London and it was printed and distributed in Germany.

From 1852 to 1862 Marx was also a foreign correspondent for the New York *Daily Tribune.* He wrote his "Critique of Political Economy" in 1859. This work served as the prologue to his later *Das Kapital.* In 1860 he studied the writings of Charles Darwin and wrote of *Natural Selection,* "it is the book that contains the natural-history basis of our philosophy" (ibid., p. 366). He sent a copy of the first volume of *Das Kapital* to Darwin and later requested Darwin's permission to dedicate volume two to him. (Darwin turned him down.)

Work on *Das Kapital* began in earnest in 1861. In 1864, in very poor health, Marx temporarily suspended work on it and devoted his failing energy to the founding of the communist *International Working Men's Association.* The first draft of *Das Kapital* was finished in 1865 and the book was finally published in Germany on September 14, 1867. His finances became somewhat stabilized and he began to join the ranks of the very class his new book condemned. During his stay in Germany for the release of *Das Kapital,* his hostess remarked to him, "I cannot think of you in a leveling society, as you have altogether aristocratic tastes and habits." Marx replied, "I cannot either. That time will come, but we will be gone by then" (ibid., pp. 201, 202).

On December 2, 1881, his beloved wife Jenny died, probably from stomach cancer, and the already-ill Marx never fully recovered from losing her. In declining health, he received the news of the death of his daughter, also named Jenny, in 1883. He went into a deep depression; his health finally failed him, and he died of an abscessed lung on March 14, 1883.

Karl Marx's personal life was an intricate pattern of conflicts, interweaving his passion for his political system with his love for his family and his middle-class upbringing. It makes a fascinating backdrop against which to picture his philosophy, his world view and his system of thought. His personal life shows that he was not a monster incarnate as some detractors would make him. Nor was he the perfect Christ-figure as others see him. He was a complicated and often contradictory man whose all-consuming interest was the philosophical system we will now consider in brief.

Philosophy

Marx never claimed to possess a "philosophy." It is true that he never developed a complete system of philosophical thought covering all of the main brances of philosophy. However, as a thinking man vitally concerned with explaining man's existence and with finding the causes for events in history, Marx was a philosopher. His disdain for traditional philosophy was related to his zeal for political and social revolution. To Marx, a person doesn't have time to be an armchair philosopher: he should be out in the streets, living his philosophy.

> Philosophy, he said, was a symptom of social malaise and would disappear when revolution put society on a healthier foundation. The young Marx thought that this would happen because revolution would "realize" philosophy, would give solid reality to the ideal phantoms of reason, justice, and liberty that philosophers in sick societies consoled themselves with. The older Marx thought that revolution would destroy philosophy, would simply make it unnecessary, by bringing men back to the study of "the real world." Study of that world is to philosophy "what sexual love is to onanism." In either case Marx never varied in the opinion that the reign of philosophy over men's minds was drawing to a close. Thus, he naturally would not have contributed to its survival by writing a "Marx-

ist philosophy" (Paul Edwards, ed., *The Encyclopedia of Philosophy*, New York: Macmillan Publishing Company, Inc., 1967, vol. 5&6, p. 173).

Regardless of Marx's dislike of traditional philosophy, he philosophized and he received great inspiration from two prominent philosophers who began writing before him.

Georg Wilhelm Hegel

Hegel (d. 1831) developed a system to explain change which is called *dialectics*. Change and progression are accomplished through a process of thesis, antithesis, and synthesis.

Hegel himself rarely used the terms *thesis, antithesis,* and *synthesis* (see Frederick Copleston, *A History of Philosophy*, Garden City, NY: Doubleday and Company, Inc., 1963, vol. 7, Part 1, p. 215). However, traditional interpretations of Hegel recognize this preoccupation with triads in Hegel's philosophy and note his debt to his predecessor, Fichte, with whom the three terms were commonplace.

There are those who protest such a generalization of Hegel's dialectic, seeing the interpretations of Marx and others as misinterpretations of Hegel (see Gustav E. Mueller, "The Hegel Legend of 'Thesis-Antithesis-Synthesis,'" in the *Journal of the History of Ideas*, vol. XIX, no. 3, June 1958, pp. 411-441; and Winfried Corduan, "Transcendentalism: Hegel," in *Biblical Errancy*, Norman Geisler, ed., Grand Rapids, MI: Zondervan Publishing Company, 1981, pp. 81-104). However, most general authorities recognize the traditional designation of Hegel's dialectic. H. B. Acton, in the *Enclyclopedia of Philosophy*, (Paul Edwards, ed., New York: Macmillan Publishing Company, Inc. 1967, vol. 3, p. 436) remarks, "It should first be noted that Hegel set out his systematic writings in dialectical triads comprising a thesis, antithesis, and synthesis." Colin Brown notes that the traditional interpretation of Hegel's dialectic must be dealt with:

> It is customary to describe Hegel's view of the outworking of Spirit as a Dialectic (which is simply another word for process or dynamic pattern) of Thesis, Antithesis and Synthesis. But it has been pointed out that although Hegel makes occasional use of these latter terms, they are in fact more characteristic

> of Fichte. However, the basic idea is there, and the notion of Dialectic is paramount. Hegel saw the Dialectic of the Spirit in everything (Colin Brown, *Philosophy and the Christian Faith*, Downers Grove, IL: InterVarsity Press, 1968, p. 121).

It is to this traditional interpretation of Hegel's dialectic, the same understanding modified by Marx, that we will address ourselves. Regardless of the "true" interpretation of Hegel's dialectic, a Christian who would critique Marx must understand Marx's interpretation of Hegel, which is compatible with the traditional interpretation.

The three dialectical principles of thesis, antithesis, and synthesis mark all of existence, all of life, all of thinking. It is not only the process through which we go to gain knowledge, it is the process through which all of existence passes. It is illustrated by Hegel's "basic triad" of *Being, Not-Being,* and *Becoming.*

> The most all-embracing concept of our minds would seem to be that of *being.* It is the least common denominator to which all things may be reduced. But pure unspecified *being* without a particular content of some sort is equivalent to nothing at all. It is indistinguishable from *not-being.* To assert, then, as a *thesis* that the Absolute is unqualified *being* is also to assert the *antithesis* of our statement, and to say that the Absolute is non-existent.
>
> Can we then find some further concept that will overcome this contradiction and prove to be a *synthesis* of the ideas of *being* and *not-being*? Hegel finds such a concept in that of *becoming.* When a thing *changes,* it *is* what is it *was not* a moment before, and it *will be* in another instant what it *is not* now. But, if it is to remain the *same* object throughout its changes, what it *is* must be somehow *identical* with what it *was not,* and with what it *will be.* In a *process* then, the seemingly mutual exclusion of *being* and *non-being* by each other is overcome in a higher synthesis (B. A. G. Fuller, *A History of Philosophy*, New York: Holt, Rinehart and Winston, 1955, vol. 2, p. 313).

Marx accepted Hegel's process of dialectics, seeing Reality as a process that can be understood by the mind and that proceeds by the dialectic of thesis, antithesis, and synthesis.

> . . . the general view, which Marx took over from Hegel, that all development, whether of thought or things, is brought about through a conflict of opposing elements or tendencies. This doctrine, as we have already seen, is two-sided. It is a description

> of the way in which things come into being, develop and behave, and it is a description of the way in which we come to learn the truth about them. For Hegel the two processes, the development of things and the discovery of truth, were aspects of the same reality; but whereas he gave logical priority to the second, Marx, holding, as we shall see, that thought is in some sense a reflection of things, emphasised the priority of the first (C. E. M. Joad, *Guide to Philosophy*, London: Victor Gollancz Ltd., 1955, p. 466).

To his triad of thesis, antithesis, and synthesis Hegel added the goal of absolute Spirit. Every process was leading to the ultimate existence, fully self-conscious Thought. The material was secondary to the spiritual.

> In Hegel the driving force of the dialectical process was engendered by the developing ideas themselves (ibid., p. 467).

However, Marx flatly rejected Hegel's Spirit-goal, adopting instead a thorough-going materialism.

> Hegel believed that by this process one eventually reached the highest synthesis possible, Absolute Spirit, which includes all possible experience. His system might be called idealistic or spiritualistic pantheism. However, Karl Marx, using the same method, concluded that the ultimate synthesis was *matter*, not Spirit, so that his system is called *dialectical materialism* (Warren Young, *A Christian Approach to Philosophy*, Grand Rapids, MI: Baker Book House, 1954, p. 33).
>
> Karl Marx received the keys to his communist kingdom from his German masters Hegel and Feuerbach. Hegel gave him the keys of the unhappy conscience and the dialectical method of analyzing history. History, according to Hegel, is the contradictory unfolding of Reason itself from less to more rational forms, to the utmost rational form of existence—fully self-conscious Thought—God Himself. . . . But Marx, his most famous follower, interpreted this action to be revolutionary action, the sole way of development for matter and man. Thus the Hegelian philosophical impulse to give a scientific analysis of history became the Marxian revolutionary action to create history (Miceli, *Atheism*, p. 96).

Marx, then was an absolute materialist (seeing ultimate reality only in matter) and believed that all process occurred through a dialectical system.

> He rejected flatly the latter's view that these characteristics of the world-process indicated that it was the teleological unfolding of a design or Idea in the experience of an Absolute Mind

> or Spirit. The behavior of the world-process, he maintained, did not suggest guidance by a moral plan or purpose. Above all, its material and physical aspects could not be reduced to conscious content and regarded as mental in their essential character. On the contrary, they could only be explained on the supposition that matter in motion, extended in space and time, and existing in and by itself, independent of any mental awareness of or reflection upon it, underlay the phenomenal world (Fuller, *Philosophy*, p. 371).

This concept is very important to remember because it forms the basis for his view of history and the future. Because only the material is fundamental, and everything (even mind) proceeds from the material, and progress can only occur through dialectic change, Marx easily concludes that class reform (dealing with the material) is man's basic priority and that such reform can occur only through revolution (dialectics). How sharply this differs from Christian teaching, where the intangible is most important, where God can and does intervene for our good, and where social reform is accomplished through the transformation of individual souls from darkness into light!

Ludwig Feuerbach

Feuerbach (d. 1872) was one of the shapers of Marx's ideas about religion. His *Essence of Christianity* (1841) reduced Christianity to man's fulfillment of his desires. There is no objective religion, no objective God, no objective Jesus Christ. All religious belief is subjective, projected from man's inner needs and desires. It is because of man's miserable existence that he feels the need to invent God.

> In other words, predicate and object of theology is man's imagination, and the religious objects, such as eternal life, God's goodness, and the like are projections of his own desires. If man had no desires, despite his fantasy, he would have no religion and no gods. . . . Religion, in short, is the true characteristic of man. It shows the feeling of man's imperfections and the desire to overcome them. But religion does not indicate that man would have cognitions of anything or anyone beyond himself (Hans Schwarz, *The Search for God*, Minneapolis, MN: Augsburg Publishing House, 1975, pp. 24, 25).
>
> Ludwig Feuerbach, with the publication of his *The Essence of Christianity*, supplied Marx with the key of a humanist, materialistic humanism. By revealing God to be the "fictitious"

> creation of man's sick conscience, Feuerbach denied the reality of God, of any transcendent, of spirit. He argued that God did not create man but that man created God out of his warped imagination. Hence only matter, nature and man exist. And man is to regain his own glory by knowing and controlling matter, of which he himself is the highest product (Miceli, *Atheism*, pp. 96, 97).

Marx went further than Feuerbach. In his typical demarcation between "philosophers" who merely observed and "revolutionaries" who acted, Marx called for revolution to bring man to the place where he no longer needed religion. He was not content to wait for man to grow out of a need for God. He was ready to join the fight himself. Marx, then, was not passive when it came to religion. The active destruction of religion and promotion of atheism was part of his plan to fulfill man through his dialectical materialism (matter is the ultimate reality and change occurs through a dialectic process).

Marx faulted him (Feuerbach) for overlooking the fact:

> that the chief thing still remained to be done. The religious projection and contradiction of the actual human situation demands a removal of the factors that make this projection necessary. According to Marx, Feuerbach was still too "pious." He had not recognized that the "religious sentiment" is not a truly anthropological phenomenon which makes man truly human. It is a *social product* and belongs to a particular form of society.
>
> . . . Thus the abolition of religion as the illusory happiness is required in order to gain real happiness. The demand to give up the illusion is the demand to give up a condition which needs illusions. "The criticism of religion is therefore in embryo the criticism of the vale of woe, the halo of which is religion." Religion is the opiate of the people and is a tool of the capitalists to comfort the suppressed working class with the prospect of a better beyond. Yet Marx demands that the working class should establish its happiness here on earth instead of projecting it into an imaginary beyond. . . . Marx is not satisfied with philosophers like Feuerbach, who have only interpreted the world in various ways. The task is to change the world (Schwarz, *Search*, pp. 25, 26).

Marx modified Feuerbach's idea as he modified Hegel's idea. He fit both into his basic materialistic world view. With the establishment of his dialectical materialism (with its roots, as we see, in Hegel and Feuerbach) he was ready to propose radical and revolutionary change into the society around him. To the downtrodden, the workers, his "proletariat," he offered dialectical materialism as a beacon of hope. To the oppresive ruling classes, the "bourgeois," dialectical materialism was to be the means of their execution.

Against Religion

Since dialectical materialism is the basis for the whole Marxist system, it is no wonder, and in fact, follows necessarily, that Marxism is thoroughly atheistic. There is no room for God in Marx's system.

Marx eagerly anticipated the day when men everywhere would recognize the face in their mirror of religion as their own.

> That is, if a man is a reality seeker and should he discover that religion is but a projection of his own imagination, he will turn to the human reality instead of worshiping the mirror that reflects it (Norman Geisler, *Philosophy of Religion*, Grand Rapids, MI: Zondervan Publishing House, 1974, p. 70).

William S. Sahakian has accurately summarized Marx's attitude toward religion:

> Marxists reject religious doctrines about spiritual values, the soul, immortality, and God, asserting that religion is an illusion, and that the illusory happiness based on it must be condemned. "Religion is the sign of the oppressed creature, the heart of the heartless world, just as it is the spirit of a spiritless situation. It is the opium of the people." God does not create man; rather, man creates invalid religion with its mythical God. Religion functions as a police force, as a bourgeois technique to dissuade the masses from revolting by promising them a better, happier existence after death than their exploiters allow them to enjoy during their lifetime on earth (William S. Sahakian, *History of Philosophy*, New York: Harper and Row, Publishers, 1968, p. 251).

Marx saw two compelling reasons to abolish religion and promote atheism: first, his materialism denied the existence of the supernatural; and second, the very structure of organized religion had, through the ages, condoned and supported the bourgeois suppression of the proletariat.

> As he saw it, Christianity had to be extirpated root and branch,

> not only because dialectical materialism denied the existence of anything but matter in motion and its products, and was therefore opposed to all supernaturalistic systems, religious and philosophical, but also because Christianity, and for that matter all religions, had not only tolerated but sanctioned the existing social and economic organization of society, which was about to be overthrown (Fuller, *Philosophy*, p. 377).

We must make this clear: abolishment of religion is an integral part of Marx's dialectical materialism.

There are some who try to synthesize Marxism and Christianity. "Liberation Theology'" proponents in various areas of South America are examples. Usually such quasi-Marxists are motivated by strong social concerns. They see inequity and suffering in the world and they want to do something about it. Too often, the Marxists are the only ones who appear to be working to relieve such suffering.

Former British communist Douglas Hyde was studying to become a missionary when he was drawn to communism in just such a way after World War I in England. He joined his first Communist sponsored Party after reading a book by a Quaker who embraced communism and extolled its virtues in *The Challenge of Bolshevism*. Young Hyde recounted his reaction to the book:

> It did for my generation of communists what the Dean of Canterbury by his books and lectures does today. It lulled my doubts about the Marxists' militant atheism. It provided a bridge by means of which the man with some religious belief could cross with a clear conscience into the camp of unbelief.
>
> The author's case was that the communists had found the Christian answer to an utterly un-Christian, bourgeois system of society. "Let the atheists of Russia speak the *language* of blasphemy: is it more than the echo of the blasphemy which has so long been embodied in the social order we uphold?"
>
> In communism this sincere Quaker found honesty of purpose, intellectual integrity, a higher morality and a system which would prepare the way for a Christianity purified and reborn. And, of course, the communists used the book for all they were worth.
>
> It was exactly what I needed at the time. It resolved a crisis for me, clarified my position and accelerated my progress towards communism. It was the link between my Christian past and my atheist future. I was able now to read with an "open mind" Engels' *Anti-Duhring*, the *A. B. C. of Communism*, the works of Lenin and others which formerly I would have rejected

because of their atheism (Douglas Hyde, *I Believed*, London: William Heinemann Ltd., 1951, pp. 22, 23).

However, as Hyde discovered, one *cannot* remain true to othodox Marxism and orthodox Christianity at the same time. Hyde quickly abandoned all faith in God and was as militantly atheistic as any other communist for more than two decades, until his disillusionment with communism drove him to Christ. Again, one cannot be an orthodox Marxist and an an orthodox Christian. Even the liberal theologian Hans Küng recognizes this when he says:

> But at this point we can hear the dogmatic response: Marxism is *necessarily atheistic*. Is this true?
>
> It is true of *orthodox Marxism*. For Marx and the classical Marxist authors, Engels, Lenin and Stalin—in their personal life, in their culture, in their system and in their practice—atheism was and remained of central importance and essentially connected with their theory of society and history. In their view, religion and science are two mutually exclusive methods of grasping reality (Hans Küng, *Does God Exist?* NY: Random House, 1978, 1980, p. 257).

For orthodox Marxism to embrace orthodox Christianity is to emasculate Marxism of its foundation: dialectical materialism. For orthodox Marxism to embrace orthodox Christianity is to emasculate Christianity of its ultimate source and sustenance in the deity, person, and work of Jesus Christ. Marx saw it this way:

> To achieve the real happiness of the people, it is necessary to abolish the illusory religious one. This involves the elimination of conditions that require such illusions. *The first step in this direction must be an attack on religion. "Criticism of religion is the prelude of all criticism"* (Padover, *Karl Marx*, p. 80).

The Soviet Communist leader Nikolai Lenin showed that he had learned well from his teacher, Marx, when his contempt for religion and religious people prompted unmentionable atrocities against thousands of innocent people, who were guilty only of believing in God. Lenin wrote:

> Every religious idea, every idea of god, every flirtation with the idea of god is unutterable vileness . . . Any person who engages in building a god, or who even tolerates the idea of god-building, disparages himself in the worst possible fashion (Nikolai Lenin, *Selected Works*, London: Lawrence and Wishart, Ltd., 1939, vol. XL, pp. 675, 676).

Some have taken various elements from Marxism and formed what they term Christian Marxism, Christian socialism, or Christian communism.

> A revised Marxism could be nonatheistic if it distinguished between dispensable and indispensable elements. The critique of religion is then no longer the precondition of all criticism. It would then no longer be—as with the classical atheistic writers—a central element in Marxism but marginal and open to modification. Such an understanding of Marxism—denounced in Moscow as "revisionist"—is found in fact today even among individual Communist parties, among individual less-orthodox party theorists, and not least in Europe and South America among those forces that are aiming at a practical alliance between Christians and Marxists. The Communist Party of Italy, like other Eurocommunist parties, rejects not only the idea of a Catholic state but also Soviet state atheism—at least for the sake of winning votes . . . (Küng, *Does God Exist?* p. 257).

Remember, though, that this is not orthodox Marxism. The Christian "socialist" *must* reject those elements of Marxism that oppose the Christian world view.

> . . . whatever his attitude to these questions, a person will in any case be taken seriously as a Christian only if Christ and not Marx is for him the ultimate, decisive authority in such questions as class struggle, use of force, terror, peace, justice, love (ibid, p. 259).

So that there can be no confusion on this point, we reiterate that atheism is an integral part of orthodox Marxism.

> It becomes evident, then, that precisely because and, in as much as it is a humanism, communism is necessarily an atheism. Atheism is not an accidental accretion to communist humanism. It is intrinsic and essential to both its creed and conduct. Atheism is as inseparable from a vital communism as the soul is inseparable from a living man. Atheism is the reverse side of communist humanism (Miceli, *Atheism*, p. 102).

In fact, Douglas Hyde expressed in his biography his belief that communist organizations that appear to be compatible with Christianity are not honest. He states that in the British Party, open atheism and hatred for the clergy was practiced before 1931, but that then there was a shift in *public* policy. He stated:

> It was all very thorough but very phoney, for we went back on none of the fundamentals; we simply put some into cold storage and found new methods of dishing up the rest.
>
> That is still the tactic today, and in the intervening years the technique has been developed to a point where the communists' public propaganda never at any time bears any relation whatsoever to their real aims as expounded in their textbooks and as taught in the privacy of their members' study classes.
>
> Communism has, in fact, become a gigantic hoax, a deliberate and total deception of the public (Hyde, *I Believed*, p. 57).

Whether or not the British Communist Party is as portrayed by Hyde, the fact remains that he perceived it that way. For almost 15 years he was a leading British communist and news editor for the communist *Daily Worker*.

Hyde did not finish his life as a communist. On the contrary, his dynamic conversion from communism to Christianity is related in his moving *I Believed*. He tells of his growing disillusionment with communism and the reawakening of his conscience, which took place over a period of years. One of the turning points came when he realized:

> It was not sufficient now to tell myself that the end justified the means. Once a Marxist begins to differentiate between right and wrong, just and unjust, good and bad, to think in terms of spiritual values, the worst has happened so far as his Marxism is concerned (ibid., p. 243).

He chronicles how he and his wife searched and how they accepted Christianity intellectually before they were reborn spiritually.

> We had come to accept the intellectual case for God, to see that without it not only Catholicism but the universe itself made nonsense. We had discovered with some surprise that the great thinkers and philosophers of the Church had made out a better case for God's existence than Marx and Engels had done for His non-existence.
>
> Yet we realised that that was not enough. Belief meant being able to *feel* the existence of the spiritual, to *know* God and not just to know *about* Him. Christians even said they loved Him, they talked to Him and listened to Him. That was still outside our experience and, in moments of depression, we feared that it would remain so (ibid., p. 248).

Hyde and his wife made personal commitments to Jesus Christ and found the faith they had yearned for. His story ends:

> I lost my communism because I had been shown something better. I did not find it easy to get to know my new God. And the love of God did not even then come automatically. Just as one has first to get to know a man or woman, and love comes later on the basis of common interest shared and intimacies exchanged, so, slowly, I came to know that love. But one thing is certain: my God has not failed (ibid., p. 303).

We are not trying to say that all communists are dishonest, immoral, and bereft of any positive characteristics or attributes. Most people are drawn to communism first because they see it as a way to help the suffering in the world, or, if they are suffering, to help themselves. Hyde, with inside knowledge, summed up the typical convert to communism:

> Most, beyond doubt, had come to communism because of the good that was in them. They had come with idealism, with anger at bad social conditions; fundamentally they had, in most cases, come because no one had ever shown them anything better. What had happened to them afterwards, as they were turned into the new Marxist men, the steel-hardened cadres which the Party makes and moulds, was another matter. I wished I could stay and make them see what I now saw, could share with them the truths which I had found. . . .
>
> Life is so much more complex, and so are men's motives, I would say that the majority who come to communism do so because, in the first instance, they are looking for a cause which will fill the void left by unbelief, or, as in my own case, an insecurely held belief which is failing to satisfy them intellectually and spiritually (ibid., pp. 274, 290).

The Loss of the Individual

A complete acceptance of Marx's dialectical materialism and theories of class struggle leads one inexorably to the denial of individual human worth. History and its march toward perfection is the Marxist god. In the struggle for the classless society, those who stand in the way must be eliminated. Absolute materialism leads to a form of practical totalitarianism. As Thomas O. Kay points out:

> If there is no God or other absolute beyond the existence of matter, then there is no source of eternal, abiding, absolute

> truth upon which an objective system of law and order can be based. All becomes relative to time and place. The expedient becomes the good and true. Matter itself is not able to provide this absolute because of its ever-changing character.
>
> Since there is no soul and since all goodness and truth are relative to time and place, it follows that there can be no abiding value attributed to man as an individual. He has no worth within himself. This makes man a tool of his environment. Furthermore it brings him under the subjection of the group. At a given moment the good of the group becomes all-embracing. The individual thus may be sacrificed for the good of the group.
>
> It is at this point that one readily observes the relationship between materialism and totalitarianism. Totalitarianism is based upon the assumption that the individual is of little or no importance and his will can be made subservient to that of another individual, a group, or the state (Kay, *Christian Answer*, p.92).

Such a totalitarianism denies the worth and freedom of the individual and cuts at the heart of the gospel message. The individual is so important to God that He sent his only begotten Son to die for our sins, that we may be reconciled to fellowship with God, on an individual basis. Marx sought to elevate man. His system only served to degrade the individual. Marx saw evil someplace out in the material world, someplace other than in the heart of free-will, moral, and personal agents. By attacking the evil he saw in society with class struggle, he hoped to eradicate evil from mankind. He and his philosophical descendents did not succeed. Sin is not man divorced from his social potential; it is man in willful alienation from himself and God.

> Sin is his self-alienation, not the projection from himself of an illusory God, as Feuerbach taught Marx. The attempt to become God in himself, by himself, is the self-alienation, a personal, subjective, self-inflicted alienation. . . . Sin corrupts, disrupts man who then corrupts and disrupts human conditions and relationships. . . .
>
> Marx makes the fundamental mistake of equating the alienation of private property, his source for all alienations, with original sin; sin is an economic evil for him; it calls for an economic saviour. The Catholic Church teaches that sin is a spiritual evil, an insult by man against God; it calls for a divine saviour, since a limited creature cannot atone for an infinite offense against an infinite Being. Yet it also calls for a human saviour, if humanity is to atone for its own offense against both

> God and man. Communist humanism holds that the redemption of man is achieved by the sufferings of the sacrificial lamb and economic saviour, the proletariat, whose crucifixion and resurrection in rebellion emancipates all men into the socialist heaven. . . . The truth of the matter is, as the Church teaches, that man is reconciled to God, his fellow man and himself by One who is at once fully Man and fully God. . . . The sufferings of proletarians are the sufferings of mere creatures; the sufferings of Christ "knock down the wall of separation" that sin erected (Miceli, *Atheism*, pp. 125, 126).

As the reader can see, there is a sharp distinction between the goal and plan of Marxism and the goal and plan of Christianity. Christianity also works toward a transformed society. This working is in two major areas. Christianity recognizes that sin, within man, is action perpetrated by personal agents. It is not some nasty by-product of social birth-pangs. Christianity seeks to change those personal agents through the life-transforming power of the Lord Jesus Christ. Then, once that personal and individual transformation has taken place, that redeemed individual shows his faith through his actions by working toward social, economic, political, and religious parity among his fellow men.

> The sharp contrast between the Communist approach and the Christian approach to the problems of society is found in comparing the life of Karl Marx with that of Lord Shaftesbury, British statesman of the nineteenth century. While Marx criticized society and fomented revolutions, Shaftesbury—an evangelical Christian—worked for the bettermen of conditions often at great personal sacrifice (Kay, *Christian Answer*, p. 19).

True freedom for mankind is possible only when the individual is considered valuable and when the root causes of injustice are removed. Such change is not brought about by violent revolution at the expense of others nor is it based on a philosophy which sees man valuable only as a member of a classless society.

> Communist humanism does not liberate man; it delivers man into his own hands to do with himself what he will; this is slavery. For, once man rejects God, he has no place to go but back into himself and there lies the agony of isolation. Thus, the revolt against God is the prelude to all serfdom. For the essence of man's freedom is that he be able to transcend himself, the material things of earth and choose to live in companion-

> ship with God. Indeed, it was in order that man might enjoy freedom that God, Absolute Liberty Himself, made man in His own image and likeness. He made him a little less than the angels. But communist humanism, in delivering man into his own hands, really renders man captive to the material world below man. Communist humanism, by ripping man down from God, the source of all freedom, makes man less than man (Miceli, *Atheism*, p. 139).

"It was for freedom that Christ set us free; therefore keep standing firm and do not be subject again to a yoke of slavery" (Galatians 5:1 NASB).

Appendix

Marxist Economics and Politics

Our aim in this chapter was to treat the religious and anti-religious aspects of Marxism. It was not our aim to deal extensively with Marx's complicated philosophical and political system as a whole. Below we have produced a short summary of the major principles of Marxism with a short critique.

Our brief description of Marxist theory will present six economic/political themes that are integral to the Marxist system and which together represent its basic thrust. These six themes include 1) dialectical materialism; 2) the four epochs of human history; 3) economic "determinism;" 4) the class struggle; 5) revolution (with a subsequent temporary proletariat dictatorship); and 6) the final "Utopia," the classless society.

1. Dialectical Materialsim

We previously discussed dialectical materialism, citing it as the foundation of Marxist thought. Dialectical materialism is, in fact, the basis of all Marxist philosophy. To Marx, dialectical materialism was the ultimate Reality. As we discussed before, Marx developed his dialectical materialism from Hegel (dialectics) and Feuerbach (materialism).

Dialectical materialism says that reality is grounded in materialism and that all progress in reality (history) occurs through a process of opposing matters clashing together and then forming a new synthesis which is progressively better than either of its forebears.

When we say that Marx was a materialist, we are not saying that he denies the relative existence of anything metaphysical, such as the mind. However, he believed that anything metaphysical, like the mind, arose *from* the material world and depended *on* the material world for its existence. He would say that matter produced mind, rather than saying that mind produced matter (or, as Christians would say, the Ultimate God, being Spirit, produced matter, the creation, from nothing).

> . . . *dialectical materialism*, that is, matter arguing with itself causes historical progress. These two polysyllables are a formidable verbal whip in the hands of the Marxist, but they are simply a shorthand for one explanation of history among many (Lester DeKoster, *Communism and Christian Faith*, Grand Rapids, MI: William B. Eerdmans Publishing Company, 1956, p. 29).

2. The Four Epochs of Human History

Marx simplistically divided all of human history into four epochs: the primitive, the ancient, the feudal, and the bourgeois (middle-class) or modern.* He felt that all previous cultures and societies could be categorized into one of the four epochs. Capitalism, the economic "god" of Marx's London residence, was the motivating force in the bourgeois epoch. Below we will mention the fifth epoch, the "classless society" which in Marx's day was a future dream.

3. Economic "Determinism"

Marxism taught that, generally speaking, economic forces controlled all of human social life. This is popularly called Marx's theory of "economic determinism." However, this term is sometimes misleading because it tends to give the impression that man has no free will and that no change can possibly come from any but an economic source. Kay summarizes:

> Marx concludes then that these economic forces determine by virtue of the dialectic the course of all human history (Kay, *Christianity*, p. 16).

However, such a statement can be misleading. Marx's economic determinism was not a rigid predestination or

---

*See Kay, *Christian Answer* p. 17.

fate. It was precisely because he believed economics could be influenced by forceful human intervention that he advocated revolution to achieve quick change.

> Dialectical materialists criticise doctrines often designated as economic determinism on the ground that they are too narrow and assert only a one-way causal influence (from economic base to other institutions), whereas causal influence, they hold, proceeds both ways. They (often) refer to their own theory as historical materialism or the materialist conception of history (Dagobert D. Runes, ed., *Dictionary of Philosophy*, Totowa, NJ: Littlefield, Adams and Company, 1977, p. 87).

In fact, his economic "determinism" was practiced during each of the four epochs of history mentioned above, with the economics of the age directing all other social functions. It was the deliberate intervention of men through revolution that brought about the end of one epoch and the beginning of the next. Marx believed that the flow of history along his fivefold pattern was inexorable. Society was bound through its economics to pass through the four epochs and eventually arrive at the fifth, the classless society and eventual freedom. The revolutionaries of each epoch were to hurry the process along. Marx saw it as the job of the communist proletariat to instigate the revolution which would terminate the epoch of the bourgeois and usher in the ultimate classless society.

Economic determinism involves Marx's whole detailed analysis of economics. Under this heading we find him discussing "the labor theory of value," i.e., a product's value is determined only by the amount of labor required to produce it.

> . . . *only labor*—manual and mental—creates value; and, what is more specifically Marx's contribution to the theory, only *socially necessary* labor creates *real value*. The fact that under capitalism the employment of labor is spent upon luxuries long before all necessities have been met, means for Marx that capitalism is not the best form for the selective use of a nation's labor force (DeKoster, *Communism*, p. 16).

The Marxist "demon" of "surplus value" also comes under this heading. "Surplus value" represents the insurmountable obstacle separating the employer and employee from peace.

> Profit, which is the motive force of capitalism, arises only out of *surplus value*, that is out of paying the workman for *less* value than his labor creates (ibid., p. 20).

When Marx talks of economic determinism, he lays out his whole view of human history. He discusses "modes of production," "property relations," "fair wages," etc. (For more than this quick overview of economic determinism, please see the books in the bibliography, especially August Thalheimer's *Introduction to Dialectical Materialism: The Marxist World-View*, NY: Covici, Friede, Publishers, 1936).

4. Class Struggle

Accepting Marx's dialectical materialism leads one to accept his view of history, which reveals his economic determinism. The acceptance of the presupposition of economic determinism draws one to the conclusion that the only way to achieve change in one's society is through class struggle. History, to Marx, is a record of continual struggle (dialectics) between different classes. He sets this forth in the *Communist Manifesto*. After its preamble, the *Communist Manifesto* opens with the words, "The history of all hitherto existing society is the history of class struggles" (Harold J. Laski, ed., *The Communist Manifesto* by Karl Marx and Friedrich Engels, NY: New American Library, 1967, p. 129).

To Marx, this class struggle has always been in existence and is present at all times in every society. However, it will not be present in the classless society Marx advocates. When dialectical conditions are just right, and the downtrodden class can take no more, the struggle will explode into revolution, paving the way for the next epoch. The final class struggle will be between the proletariat (working class) and the bourgeois (commercial class).

> . . . the current class struggle in capitalist society would be the last and was by far the greatest of all. The proletariat (working class) was the antithesis of the bourgeois (commercial or middle-class) capitalist and would eventually bring about the downfall of capitalist society and the establishment of a new society on the basis of the new modes of production (Kay, *Christian Answer*, p. 17).

5. Revolution

As mentioned earlier, Marx saw the bridge between two epochs of history as revolution, triggered by class struggle. Such revolution is necessary and vital to the evolution of society toward the eventual, economically determined, communist state of the classless society.

> Although Marx held that the inevitable outcome of history was the emergence of the communist society, he felt that because of the great problems in this last stage there was a role which man could play in aiding the course of history (ibid., p. 17).

The *Communist Manifesto* was Marx's blueprint for the leadership of the coming revolution. In it he and Engels laid down their plans for overthrowing capitalism and ushering in history's final epoch, the classless society. As with the other themes of Marxism, note that the concept of revolution is a *necessary* consequence of Marx's dialectical materialism. Revolution *must* occur.

Marx recognized that after this final revolution not everyone (namely, the bourgeois) would welcome the classless society. In addition, the entire capitalistic system, with its modes of production, would have to be dismantled and retooled to fit the classless society. During this "short" interim, it would be necessary to have a proletariat dictatorship. This was seen as a temporary and necessary hardship that all proletariats would welcome because of the vital work the dictatorship would do to develop the final classless society.

6. The Classless Society

The final and fifth epoch of human social history would be the classless society, the Marxist "Utopia," its "heaven." In this ideal, no-class society, hard-won by thousands of years of class struggle, revolution, and temporary dictatorship, there would be no class struggles. With no class struggles, there would be no end to the paradise.

The communist society would be the classless society. (Remember that what we call "communist countries" today have not yet reached this classless state. They are still in the "temporary" proletariat dictatorship.) The communist society would have abolished private ownership, the "stifling" family unit, the delusion of religion, and all other "capitalistic" institutions. There will be no need for government or law. The natural law of dialectical materialism will have reached its goal in producing the perfect society.

> What would become of history itself, which was propelled by the energies released by class struggle? Strictly speaking, it

> would cease. Time would pass, of course, but the only economic changes to be reflected in society would be those leading to ever greater production, ever more leisure for all, and so history in the present tense would, with the dialectic, be transformed into universal tranquility and peace. The economic law would be, in the words of Marx: "From each according to his ability, and to each according to his need." The millennium would be ushered in, on earth and in time. Evil, which is the fruit of class struggle, would be done away. The development of science would bring man ever closer to the control of natural catastrophe. Art and culture could flourish. A temporal heaven would have been brought to earth (DeKoster, *Communism*, p. 34).

This is the final of the six major themes of Marxism.

General Critique

Rather than picking Marxism's themes apart piece by piece, we will offer here a general critique of the system. We urge the reader to obtain a comprehensive critique of Marxism by referring to the books in the bibliography, especially to William O. Kay's *The Christian Answer to Communism* and Lester DeKoster's *Communism and Christian Faith*.

From a Christian perspective, the most ominous flaw in Marxism is its broad anti-supernaturalistic foundation. One cannot accept thorough-going and classical dialectical materialism and orthodox Christianity at the same time.

Marx's economic theory is simplistic and thus inadequate, unable to correctly diagnose contemporary economic ills or correctly prognosticate concerning the future of economics. He overemphasizes the role of economic factors in the course of history.

His description of history and how it advances is also inadequate. The historical divisions are artificial and no longer supportable in any real sense when one views contemporary understandings of history.

Orthodox Marxism ignores the fact that some change does take place without struggle, and that often, when change takes place as a result of struggle, it does not result in an entire economy being completely gutted and replaced.

Orthodox Marxism has no guideline for limiting the duration of the "temporary" proletariat dictatorship after the final revolution. Are there perhaps Russians who feel that a "temporary" dictatorship which spans their whole lifetimes is no better than a "permanent" dictatorship?

Orthodox Marxism also presupposes that man is basically good. Marxism sees evil as a product of a sick society. Cure the society (or shoot it and replace it with a new one) and evil disappears. Human history and God's Word, the Bible, say differently.

Finally, Marxism ignores the greatest human freedom there is: personal freedom. Economic freedom is not the most important freedom of all. God has given mankind personal freedom, the freedom to choose his own destiny. This personal freedom has been recognized and enhanced in those societies that are politically and religiously democratic.

> (Marx) also held that it was society that determined the consciousness of man rather than man of society. But what is society without the individual? Marx has given us a rationale that is non-existent in actuality (Kay, *Christian Answer*, p. 19).

We shall conclude this brief look at Marxist theory with two quotes which appear as fitting criticisms of a powerful system that is, nevertheless, inadequate to meet men's needs. The first quote is from a modern communist who classifies himself as an "unorthodox" Marxist. Here is his analysis of classical Marxism:

> The orthodox theory does little to explain the complex dynamics of human behavior and personality. Historical materialism, the orthodox theory of history and social change, focuses our attention on too few needs, makes a fetish of production, and overlooks too many aspects of capitalist everyday life. It seeks fundamental contradictions where none are to be found. It misses the complex dynamics of how societies maintain their stability, and of how revolution occurs as well.
>
> The orthodox Marxism which is still quite prevalent and at the root of almost all socialist organizational activity, insufficiently recognizes the multiplicity of groups and issues central to social change. Economic aspects continually exclude concerns of a more social and cultural nature; ownership relations exclude more complex sex, race, and authority relations. In short, orthodox Marxism is vulgar. It clings to so-called fundamentals and in doing so misses the broader picture. The modern orthodox Marxist sees reality through a set of insufficient concepts. Reality's fullness is obscured. Facts are made to conform with the theory rather than the reverse. The per-

> son as subject/object of history is lost to view (Michael Albert and Robin Hahnel, *UnOrthodox Marxism*, Boston, MA: South End Press, 1978, p. 6).

Our final quote is from the astute ex-communist leader and editor, Douglas Hyde:

> It has been taken for granted by those attracted to communism that the man who can see and denounce the evils of a social system is thereby qualified also to lay down the lines of a better one and, in due course, to administer it. Experience shows that there is little to warrant this assumption. For one evil thing to attack another is normal enough. It does not make either the attacker or that which is attacked less evil because one is attacked by the other.
>
> The communist may be able to put his finger on what is bad in our society but only the Christian is fitted to expound the good (Hyde, *I Believed*, p. 300).

Marxism Extended Bibliography

Albert, Michael and Robin Hahnel, *UnOrthodox Marxism*. Boston: South End Press, 1978.

Andrews, William G., ed., *European Political Institutions*. Princeton, NJ: D. Van Nostrand Company, Inc., 1962, 1966.

Avey, Albert E., *Handbook in the History of Philosophy*. NY: Harper and Row, Publishers, 1954, 1961.

Angeles, Peter A., *Dictionary of Philosophy*. NY: Harper and Row, Publishers, 1981.

Bottomore, T. B., trans., *Karl Marx: Selected Writings in Sociology and Social Philosophy*. NY: McGraw-Hill Book Company, 1956.

____________, trans., *Karl Marx: Early Writings*. NY: McGraw-Hill Book Company, 1963.

Brown, Colin, *Philosophy and the Christian Faith*. Downers Grove, IL: InterVarsity Press, 1968.

Carlebach, Julius, *Karl Marx and the Radical Critique of Judaism*. London: Routledge and Kegan Paul, 1978.

Dean, Thomas, *Post-Theistic Thinking*. Philadelphia: Temple University Press, 1975.

DeKoster, Lester, *Communism and Christian Faith*. Grand Rapids, MI: William B. Eerdmans Publishing Company, 1956.

Dupre, Louis, *The Philosophical Foundations of Marxism*. NY: Harcourt, Brace and World, Inc., 1966.

Edwards, Paul, ed., *The Encyclopedia of Philosophy, 8 Vols.* NY: Macmillan Publishing Company, Inc., 1967.

Encyclopaedia Britannica III, Macropaedia, "Philosophy of Religion." Chicago, IL: William Benton, Publisher, 1978, vol. 15.

Flew, Antony, *A Dictionary of Philosophy*. NY: St. Martin's Press, 1982.

Fuller, B. A. G., *A History of Philosophy*. NY: Holt, Rinehart and Winston, 1955.

Geisler, Norman, *Philosophy of Religion*. Grand Rapids, MI: Zondervan Publishing House, 1974.

Hyde, Douglas, *I Believed*. London: William Heinemann, Ltd., 1951.

Joad, C. E. M., *Guide to Philosophy*. London: Victor Gollancz, Ltd., 1955.

Kamenka, Eugene, *The Ethical Foundations of Marxism*. London: Routledge and Kegan Paul, 1962, 1972.

Kay, Thomas O., *The Christian Answer to Communism*. Grand Rapids, MI: Zondervan Publishing House, 1961.

Koren, Henry J., *Marx and the Authentic Man*. Pittsburgh, PA: Duquesne University Press, 1967.

Küng, Hans, *Does God Exist?* NY: Random House, 1980.

Laski, Harold J., *The Communist Manifesto by Karl Marx and Friedrich Engels*. NY: New American Library, 1967.

Lee, Francis Nigel, *Communist Eschatology*. Nutley, NJ: The Craig Press, 1974.

Lenin, Nikolai, *Selected Works*. London: Lawrence and Wisehart Ltd., 1939, Vol. XL.

McFadden, Charles J., *The Philosophy of Communism*. New York: Benziger Bros., 1963.

McLellan, David, *Marxism after Marx*. Boston: Houghton Mifflin Company, 1979.

Marsden, George and Frank Roberts, *A Christian View of History?* Grand Rapids, MI: William B. Eerdmans Publishing Company, 1975.

Miceli, Vincent P., *The Gods of Atheism*. New Rochelle, NY: Arlington House, 1971.

Montgomery, John Warwick, *The Shape of the Past*. Minneapolis: Bethany Fellowship, Inc., 1975.

__________, *Where is History Going?* Minneapolis: Bethany Fellowship, Inc., 1969.

Niebuhr, Reinhold, *Marx and Engels on Religion*. NY: Schocken Books, 1964.

North, Gary, *Marx's Religion of Revolution*. Nutley, NJ: The Craig Press, 1968.

Padover, Saul K., *Karl Marx: An Intimate Biography*. NY: New American Library, 1978, 1980 (abridged ed.).

Parsons, Howard L., *Humanism and Marx's Thought*. Springfield, IL: Charles C. Thomas Publisher, 1971.

Payne, Robert, *The Unknown Karl Marx*. NY: New York University Press, 1971.

Runes, Dagobert D., *Dictionary of Philosophy*. Totowa, NJ: Littlefield, Adams and Company, 1977.

__________, *Philosophy for Everyman*. Totowa, NJ: Littlefield, Adams and Company, 1974.

Sahakian, William S., *History of Philosophy*. NY: Harper and Row, Publishers, 1968.

__________, and Mabel Lewis Sahakian, *Ideas of the Great Philosophers*. NY: Harper and Row, Publishers, 1966.

Schwarz, Hans, *The Search for God*. Minneapolis: Augsburg Publishing House, 1975.

Stumpf, Samuel Enoch, *Socrates to Sartre: A History of Philosophy*. NY: McGraw-Hill Book Company, 1966.

__________, *Philosophy: History and Problems*, 2nd edition (new title). NY: McGraw-Hill Book Company, 1966.

Taylor, A. J. P., *Karl Marx/Friedrich Engels: The Communist Manifesto*. NY: Penguin Books, 1967.

Thalheimer, August, *Introduction to Dialectical Materialism: The Marxist World-View*. NY: Covici, Friede, Publishers, 1936.

Titus, Harold H., *Living Issues in Philosophy*. NY: American Book Company, 1964.

Trueblood, D. Elton, *Philosophy of Religion*. Grand Rapids, MI: Baker Book House, 1957.

Tucker, Robert C., *Philosophy and Myth in Karl Marx*. Cambridge: University Press, 1972.

Young, Warren C., *A Christian Approach to Philosophy*. Grand Rapids, MI: Baker Book House, 1954.

CHAPTER THREE

Secular Humanism

One of the most organized, most challenging and most clearly non-Christian philosophies of today is *secular humanism*. It is ably represented and defended by a core of prominent scientists and philosophers at the forefront of new scientific and philosophical thought. Secular humanism has its own meetings, its own "clergy" of spokesmen, its own "creed" called *The Humanist Manifesto*, and its own goals toward which it desires all of humanity to work. Because of its cohesive world view and strong threat to biblical Christianity, it needs to be examined and answered in this book.

First, let's examine some popular ideas of what humanism can represent. The term *humanism* by itself is not automatically anti-God or pro-God, as many have tried so often to maintain. Historically, during Renaissance times, the word emphasized the importance of man, not to the exclusion of God, but simply with little emphasis on God.

Sometimes humanism is defined as the study of the worth and dignity of man as such worth is given him by God. As Christians, we must be careful not to build a false case about all use of the word humanism and then attempt to refute that false case. In fact, this is what some secular humanist writers do when they unfairly paint a caricature of Christianity and then attempt to tear that down.

We will make a working definition of secular humanism, adapting it from the ancient Greek philosopher Protagoras, who said, "Man is the measure of all things." Today this view holds that man is the ultimate standard by which all life is measured and judged. Thus values, law, justice, good, beauty, and right and wrong all are to be judged by man-made rules with no credence to either God or the Bible. We identify this as secular (non-theistic) humanism (in distinction to the ambiguous and broad term humanism).

Secular humanism is a collection of ideas which bind together into a coherent system. Because of this, some humanistic ideas can affect and be adapted to many different disciplines such as existentialism and communism. Thus, while we can define humanism generally, we will be careful to recognize that there is some measure of latitude in the system and our definition can be modified as necessary. Peter Angeles, in his *Dictionary of Philosophy*, defines philosophical humanism as follows:

> A philosophy that (a) regards the rational individual as the highest value; (b) considers the individual to be the ultimate source of value; and (c) is dedicated to fostering the individual's creative and moral development in a meaningful and rational way without reference to concepts of the supernatural (Peter Angeles, *Dictionary of Philosophy*, NY: Harper & Row, Publishers, 1981, p. 116).

As rational theists and evangelical Christians, our argument with secular humanism centers on its denial of the supernatural, especially as that precludes any idea of God. In this chapter we will examine, from secular humanistic literature itself, the main tenets of secular humanism and give brief Christian responses to its sweeping claims. By defining secular humanism, we as Christians see the need for evaluating it. Rejection of God, the Bible and the gospel of Jesus Christ compels us to defend the gospel through open discussion, evaluation, and refutation of these tenets of secular humanism. Support of this creed denies the heart of Christianity. (We refer the reader to the chapter on atheism for a closer look at arguments against the existence of God).

Historical Perspective

One can trace the roots of modern secular humanism back to the renewed emphasis on man during the Renaissance. This revival of classical learning and emphasis on man did not exclude God as man's Maker, but it focused attention away from Him, as man made great strides on his own.

Later God was de-emphasized to the point where He was no longer seen as an intimate worker in creation and Father to mankind, and before long, deism became a prominent view. Deism affirmed belief in God, but a God who was not involved in the affairs of men. Deism soon gave way to naturalism, a world view which dismissed God completely from the scene.

One can trace secular humanism from the Renaissance to the present. Humanism entered the nineteenth century through the French philosopher, Comte, who was committed to the secularization of science, and through British utilitarianism via English deism. These serve as a backdrop for twentieth century naturalism and pragmatism. Through such men as Schiller and especially Dewey, the modern tenets of secular humanism began to take their expressed form.

Today this self-centered system of ideas exerts influence in all of our lives. Its assumptions and dogmas continue to be adopted by more and more people, and as a result, many secular humanist organizations are in existence both in Europe and in America, some of which have been around for a long time. Two prominent organizations, *The American Humanist Association* and *The British Humanist Association*, are both front-runners in the secular humanist cause. Another secular humanist-oriented organization is *The Aspen Institute for Humanistic Studies* (see *The Aspen Idea* by Sidney Hyman, Norman, OK: University of Oklahoma Press, 1975). *The Aspen Institute* is a motivator for thought and action on cultural issues affecting man and society. Committed to and rooted in a secular humanistic approach, it seeks solutions to local, national, and international problems. Another organization is *The Sex Information and Education Council* (see *The Siecus Circle: A Humanist Revolution*, Claire Chambers, Belmont, MA: Western Islands Publishing Company, 1977). *The Sex Information and Education Council* is humanistic in its outlook and policy. The periodical *The Humanist*, a bimonthly publication, is a leading outlet in America for secular humanist doctrine.

The Humanist Manifesto I

Unlike some of the quasi-religious secular movements we discuss in this book, secular humanism is a well-organized movement with unified beliefs, goals, and presuppositions. More than most modern movements, it represents an organized corporate unity.

In 1933 secular humanists, drawn together by like beliefs, ideas, and dreams, drafted a manifesto which became the creed of secular humanism. Drafter and philosopher Paul Kurtz explains the background of the *Humanist Manifesto I*:

> In the twentieth century, humanist awareness has developed at a rapid pace; yet it has to overcome powerful anti-humanist forces that seek to destroy it.
>
> In 1933 a group of thirty-four liberal humanists in the United States defined and enunciated the philosophical and religious principles that seemed to them fundamental. They drafted *Humanist Manifesto I*, which for its time was a radical document. It was concerned with expressing a general religious and philosophical outlook that rejected orthodox and dogmatic positions and provided meaning and direction, unity and purpose to human life. It was committed to reason, science, and democracy (Paul Kurtz, ed., *Humanist Manifesto I and II*, Buffalo, NY: Prometheus Books, 1973, p. 3).

The Humanist Manifesto I reflected the general optimism of the time immediately after World War I. Mankind was convinced that it had ably weathered, in the war, the greatest evil imaginable, and that the future perfecting of humanity was now possible. Mankind had proved that it could triumph over evil.

In summary, the *Humanist Manifesto I* dealt with 15 major themes, or convictions, of secular humanism. It asserted that the universe was self-existing and not created; that man is a result of a continuous natural process; that mind is a projection of body and nothing more; that man is molded mostly by his culture; that there is no supernatural; that man has outgrown religion and any idea of God; that man's goal is the development of his own personality, which ceases to exist at death; that man will continue to develop to the point where he will look within himself and to the natural world for the solution to all of his problems; that all institutions and/or religions that in some way impede this "human development" must be changed; that socialism is the ideal form of economics; and that all of mankind deserves to share in the fruits from following the above tenets.

The conclusion to the *Humanist Manifesto I* clearly reflects the anti-supernatural and optimistic, self-centered aims of its signers:

> Though we consider the religious forms and ideas of our fathers no longer adequate, the quest for the good life is still the central task for mankind. Man is at last becoming aware that he alone is responsible for the realization of the world of his dreams, that he has within himself the power for its achievement. He must set intelligence and will to the task (Kurtz, *Manifesto*, p. 10).

The Humanist Manifesto II

World War II and Adolph Hitler rudely contradicted the unmitigated optimism of the secular humanists who signed the 1933 *Manifesto*. Not only had World War I failed to rout evil, but evil had reared its ugly head much more powerfully through the Nazi atrocities of World War II. Having rejected the supernatural and a higher Judge in favor of the basic goodness and perfectibility of man, the secular humanists turned toward modifying their previous statements. Drafters Paul Kurtz and Edwin H. Wilson explained the need for a new *Manifesto*:

> It is forty years since *Humanist Manifesto I* (1933) appeared. Events since then make that earlier statement seem far too optimistic. Nazism has shown the depthsof brutality of which humanity is capable. Other totalitarian regimes have suppressed human rights without ending poverty. Science has sometimes brought evil as well as good. Recent decades have shown that inhuman wars can be made in the name of peace. The beginnings of police states, even in democratic societies, widespread government espionage, and other abuses of power by military, political, and industrial elites, and the continuance of unyielding racism, all present a different and difficult social outlook. In various societies, the demands of women and minority groups for equal rights effectively challenge our generation.
>
> As we approach the twenty-first century, however, an affirmative and hopeful vision is needed. Faith, commensurate with advancing knowledge, is also necessary. In the choice between despair and hope, humanists respond in this *Humanist Manifesto II* with a positive declaration for times of uncertainty.

> As in 1933, humanists still believe that traditional theism, especially faith in the prayer-hearing God, assumed to love and care for persons, to hear and understand their prayers, and to be able to do something about them, is an unproved and outmoded faith. Salvationism, based on mere affirmation, still appears as harmful, diverting people with false hopes of heaven hereafter. Reasonable minds look to other means for survival.
>
> Those who sign *Humanist Manifesto II* disclaim that they are setting forth a binding credo; their individual views would be stated in widely varying ways. The statement is, however, reaching for vision in a time that needs direction. It is social analysis in an effort at consensus. New statements should be developed to supersede this, but for today it is our conviction that humanism offers an alternative that can serve present day needs and guide humankind toward the future (ibid., p. 13).

The thrust of the new *Manifesto*, published in 1973, is much more aggressive than that of the first. No longer content to let basically good mankind evolve naturally toward his zenith, the secular humanists now have a consuming drive to help accomplish that transformation as quickly as possible, thwarting the evil of the few evil men. The introduction to the resolutions in the second creed declares:

> Humanity, to survive, requires bold and daring measures. We need to extend the uses of scientific method, not renounce them, to fuse reason with compassion in order to build constructive social and moral values. Confronted by many possible futures, we must decide which to pursue. The ultimate goal should be the fulfillment of the potential for growth in each human personality—not for the favored few, but for all of humankind. Only a shared world and global measures will suffice.
>
> A humanist outlook will tap the creativity of each human being and provide the vision and courage for us to work together. This outlook emphasizes the role human beings can play in their own spheres of action. The decades ahead call for dedicated, clear-minded men and women able to marshal the will, intelligence, and cooperative skills for shaping a desirable future. Humanism can provide the purpose and inspiration that so many seek; it can give personal meaning and significance to human life (ibid., pp. 14, 15).

Humanism is the new religion, the new God who gives meaning to life as the old one never could. This is the interloper into divinity which the Christian must challenge and answer.

The Secular Humanist Creed

The belief system of secular humanists is clearly spelled out in the *Humanist Manifesto II*. It is very easy to see just what the humanists have committed themselves to and just what they desire for us as Christians to embrace instead of our Lord and Savior, Jesus Christ. In order to understand and deal with the claims of humanism in such a small space, we have elected to reproduce each resolution of *Manifesto II* and below it our comments from an evangelical perspective. These resolutions may be found on pages 13-24 of the previously mentioned *Humanist Manifesto I and II*, edited by Paul Kurtz. This is not meant to be an exhaustive examination and refutation of secular humanism, but it will serve to acquaint the reader with humanist thought and will give the reader a Christian background to the subject. Since much of *Manifesto II* deals with a denial of the existence of God and the supernatural, the reader is referred to the chapter on atheism and its bibliography of Christian books for further information. The subject will not be dealt with extensively here.

A study of *Manifesto II* reveals that its 17 propositions can be categorized into six groups and we will present them within those groupings of Religion, Philosophy, Mankind, Society, One-World Government, and Science.

Religion

Religion is the topic of the first two resolutions. We quote a portion of the first resolution and the entire (shorter) second resolution:

> First: . . . We believe, however, that traditional dogmatic or authoritarian religions that place revelation, God, ritual, or creed above human needs and experience do a disservice to the human species. Any account of nature should pass the tests of scientific evidence; in our judgment, the dogmas and myths of traditional religions do not do so. Even at this late date in human history, certain elementary facts based upon the critical use of scientific reason have to be restated. We find insufficient evidence for belief in the existence of a supernatural; it is either meaningless or irrelevant to the question of the survival and fulfillment of the human race. As non-theists, we begin with humans not God, nature not deity. Nature may indeed be broader and deeper than we now know; any new discoveries, however, will but enlarge our knowledge of the natural. . . .
>
> But we can discover no divine purpose or providence for the human species. While there is much that we do not know,

> humans are responsible for what we are or will become. No deity will save us; we must save ourselves.
>
> Second: Promises or immortal salvation or fear of eternal damnation are both illusory and harmful. They distract humans from present concerns, from self-actualization, and from rectifying social injustices. Modern science discredits such historic concepts as the "ghost in the machine" and the "separable soul." Rather, science affirms that the human species is an emergence from natural evolutionary forces. As far as we know, the total personality is a function of the biological organism transacting in a social and cultural context. There is no credible evidence that life survives the death of the body. We continue to exist in our progeny and in the way that our lives have influenced others in our culture.
>
> Traditional religions are surely not the only obstacles to human progress. Other ideologies also impede human advance. Some forms of political doctrine, for instance, function religiously, reflecting the worst features of orthodoxy and authoritarianism, especially when they sacrifice individuals on the altar of Utopian promises. Purely economic and political viewpoints, whether capitalist or communist, often function as religious and ideological dogma. Although humans undoubtedly need economic and political goals, they also need creative values by which to live.

The world view of humanism, as expressed by these first two tenets, is diametrically opposed to Christianity. While the humanists start and end with man, the Bible starts and ends with God. It was God who was in the beginning (Genesis 1:1, John 1:1-3), not impersonal, self-creating nature, from which man gradually evolved. The Bible consistently teaches that it is upon the infinite God that this finite world depends for its existence. For primordial, nonintelligent mass to produce human intelligence assumes, contrary to reason, that an effect is greater than its cause. To account for that human intelligence by a higher intelligence in whose image the human was made, and who sustains the very life of the human and his world, is reasonable, and biblical. When the apostle Paul argued with the Greek philosophers of his day he testified about this sustaining God:

> The God who made the world and all things in it, since He is both Lord of heaven and earth, does not dwell in temples made with hands; neither is He served by human hands, as though He needed anything, since He Himself gives to all life

> and breath and all things;. . . for in Him we live and move and exist, as even some of your own poets have said, 'For we also are His offspring' (Acts 17: 24-28, NASB).

For the humanists to blithely dismiss all religious philosophy and all evidence in support of the existence of God in two simple propositions does not settle the matter of God's existence. As evangelical Christians we believe that our reasoning ability was given to us by God, in whose image we were created, and that responsible use of our reasoning ability to understand the world around us can lead us to sound evidence for the existence of God. Christian philosopher Richard Purtill expressed it this way:

> . . . if we begin to ask fundamental questions about the universe, and follow the argument where it leads us, then it will lead us to belief in God; that if we examine the evidence of history and of human experience, we will be compelled to acknowledge that the only satisfactory explanation of the evidence leads us to Christianity. Such Christians acknowledge that there is still a gap between intellectual assent and commitment to a Christian way of life, but they believe that reason is neither opposed to such a commitment nor irrelevant to it—rather, it is the best possible ground for it (Richard Purtill, *C. S. Lewis's Case for the Christian Faith*, San Francisco: Harper and Row, Publishers, 1981, pp. 12, 13).

Our chapter on atheism deals with this subject more in depth, and we also refer the reader to our other works, *Evidence That Demands a Verdict*, *The Resurrection Factor*, and *More Than a Carpenter* by Josh McDowell, and *Answers* and *Reasons* by Josh McDowell and Don Stewart. We believe that God has given sufficient evidence as to His existence and His purpose in this world for man.

The French philosopher Pascal stated the matter plainly:

> The evidence of God's existence and his gift is more than compelling, but those who insist that they have no need of Him or it will always find ways to discount the offer (Blaise Pascal, *Pense's No. 430*, translated by H. F. Stewart, NY: Random House, n.d., n.p.).

When *Manifesto II* says that it can find no design or purpose or providence for the human species, it devaluates man to a level below that on which God places Him as His highest creation. The humanists pretend to esteem the human being above all else. In reality, as *Manifesto II* shows, the humanist takes away all worth from mankind. Unless our worth is rooted and grounded in something objective and outside ourselves, we are of value only to ourselves, and can never rise above the impermanence of our own short lives. The God of Christianity is outside our finite and transitory universe and His love for us gives us a value which transcends not only ourselves but our finite universe as well.

Humanist Manifesto II states that we must save ourselves. While we believe this statement was made somewhat tongue-in-cheek, since humanists do not believe man needs saving from anything, we do still need to comment on the statement. We believe it is not possible for an individual to save himself in all circumstances. In fact, given the biblical definition of salvation, it is an operation undertaken because the indiviudual *cannot* help himself. While we would grant that a man could "save himself" from falling after a slip by grabbing a railing, for example, it is not always possible. Picture a man in the middle of a large lake. He has fallen from his boat, which is now hopelessly out of reach. He has been in the frigid water for two hours. He can no longer keep himself afloat. His body temperature is falling rapidly. He is becoming delirious. Would he find solace and genuine help in a bystander's admonition to "save himself"? Of course not. Without *outside* intervention, he will die. The spiritual (moral) condition of man is such that he is past the point of "saving himself." He needs *outside* intervention. Christians believe that intervention is from God. He alone is able to save man.

If there really is a God, and if man really is in the state of decay in which he finds himself because of his deliberate sin (offense) against God, then he must turn to God for his salvation. To use another human illustration, if one man hits another, he cannot rectify the situation by saying, "So-and-So isn't angry with me anymore for my hitting him, because I forgave myself." No, So-and-So is the one offended, and he is the only one who can extend forgiveness to his attacker. That is the biblical picture of sin and salvation. Ephesians 2:8-10 reminds us:

> For by grace you have been saved through faith; and that not of yourselves, it is the gift of God; not as a result of works, that no one should boast. For we are His workmanship, created

> in Christ Jesus for good works, which God prepared beforehand, that we should walk in them (NASB).

Contrary to humanist declarations, Christianity gives true worth and dignity to man and secular humanism makes all human dignity subjective and self-centered. Francis Schaeffer comments:

> I am convinced that one of the great weaknesses in evangelical preaching in the last few years is that we have lost sight of the biblical fact that man is wonderful. We have seen the unbiblical humanism which surrounds us, and, to resist this in our emphasis on man's lostness, we have tended to reduce man to a zero. Man is indeed lost, but that does not mean he is nothing. We *must* resist humanism, but to make man a zero is neither the right way nor the best way to resist it....
>
> In short, therefore, man is not a cog in a machine; he is not a piece of theater; he really can influence history. From the biblical viewpoint, *man is lost, but great* (Francis Schaeffer, *Death in the City*, Downers Grove, IL: InterVarsity Press, 1969, pp. 80, 81).

Secular humanism rejects the idea of life after death, dogmatically asserting that it is impossible to prove. On the contrary, the resurrection of Jesus Christ from the dead is a fact of history, verifiable by standard historical tests. His resurrection becomes the seal and the hope of every Christian. In addition to the works previously cited in what we have written before on this subject, we here quote Michael Green:

> The evidence points unmistakably to the fact that on the third day Jesus rose. This was the conclusion to which a former Chief Justice of England, Lord Darling, came. At a private dinner party the talk turned to the truth of Christianity, and particularly to a certain book dealing with the resurrection. Placing his fingertips together, assuming a judicial attitude, and speaking with a quiet emphasis that was extraordinarily impressive, he said, 'We, as Christians, are asked to take a very great deal on trust; the teachings, for example, and the miracles of Jesus. If we had to take all on trust, I, for one, should be skeptical. The crux of the problem of whether Jesus was, or was not, what He proclaimed Himself to be, must surely depend upon the truth or otherwise of the resurrection. On that greatest point we are not merely asked to have faith. In its favour as living truth there exists such an overwhelming evidence, positive and negative, factual and circumstantial, that no intelligent jury in the world could fail to bring in a verdict that the resurrec-

tion story is true' (Michael Green, *Man Alive*, Downers Grove, IL: InterVarsity Press, 1968, pp. 53, 54).

Philosophy

The second major division in *Manifesto II* covers propositions three and four and relates mostly to philosophy.

> Third: We affirm that moral values derive their source from human experience. Ethics is *autonomous and situational*, needing no theological or ideological sanction. Ethics stems from human need and interest. To deny this distorts the whole basis of life. Human life has meaning because we create and develop our futures. Happiness and the creative realization of human needs and desires, individually and in shared enjoyment, are continuous themes of humanism. We strive for the good life, here and now. The goal is to pursue life's enrichment despite debasing forces of vulgarization, commercialization, bureaucratization, and dehumanization.
>
> Fourth: Reason and intelligence are the most effective instruments that humankind possesses. There is no substitute: neither faith nor passion suffices in itself. The controlled use of scientific methods, which have transformed the natural and social sciences since the Renaissance, must be extended further in the solution of human problems. But reason must be tempered by humility, since no group has a monopoly of wisdom or virtue. Nor is there any guarantee that all problems can be answered. Yet critical intelligence, infused by a sense of human caring, is the best method that humanity has for resolving problems. Reason should be balanced with compassion and empathy and the whole person fulfilled. Thus, we are not advocating the use of scientific intelligence independent of or in opposition to emotion, for we believe in the cultivation of feeling and love. As science pushes back the boundary of the known, one's sense of wonder is continually renewed, and art, poetry, and music find their places, along with religion and ethics.

These two tenets of secular humanism are concerned with philosophy, or the way the world is viewed. They are specifically concerned with ethics first and then with reason. Again, developing from the secular humanistic presupposition of the autonomy and self-sufficiency of man, these two humanistic concerns are wholly exhausted within the framework of man.

The humanists are right to point out that their ethics (morals) are situational. Since they are based in and come forth from the individual, they are necessarily self-centered and subjective. They have no objective basis or root. On the surface, this appears to promote one's idea of the importance and power of man.

However, upon closer examination, we find flaws with this view. If moral values are determined from human experience, there is no objective basis for calling anything right or wrong. There is no such thing as intrinsic good or intrinsic evil. Whether something is good or not depends on the context of the individual or the group of like-minded individuals—the society. On this basis, could we condemn the society of Nazi Germany for judging the moral value of Jewish life as worthless? Would we have the right to call it bad? What if happiness in one society is eating one's enemy instead of convincing him to surrender?

Because humanism does not offer any absolute value system, mankind has no absolute system of right and wrong. In such an instance, why should I believe and accept the value system of the group (society) of men who drafted and signed *Manifesto II*? What compelling reason can they give me for accepting their dogmatic ethical assertion that "vulgarization, commercialization, bureaucratization, and dehumanization" are "debasing?" What if I happen to believe that it is *good* to promote vulgarization, commercialization, bureaucratization, and dehumanization?

Christianity asserts that there is absolute good and absolute evil. Our moral values are patterned after the nature and attributes of our creator, God. He is the absolute standard by which everything else is judged. Hitler's Germany was wrong because our God has declared that all human life is sacred and of equal value, whether it is the human life of a Jew, a German, and unborn child, or a senile old man, crippled and bedridden.

The fourth article of *Manifesto II* concerns the role of reason in determining man's future. We believe that the main fault with this view of reason, that it can direct all human development, is that the humanist has no valid reason for accepting his own reason.

If mankind is actually a product of long evolutionary development from simpler life forms, having its ultimate origin in impersonal matter, how can a man know today that he is reasonable? Is impersonal matter a sufficient cause for personal mind (reason)? And even if this mindless

Nature did produce a self-cognizant (personal) being, how could that self-cognizant being know that his thinking process is rational, i.e., reasonable?

The Christian does not see reason rising from within man, the biological machine. The Christian believes that man's reason was created by God and patterned after (in the image of) God. Man's reason can make sense of the world in which he lives because someone who is outside this world has equipped him with the critical apparatus necessary.

Although science and technology, manipulated by man's reason, have made amazing strides in solving problems, they have not answered the ultimate questions of life. They may be able, some day, to answer the "how" of life. They can never answer the "why" of life. Os Guiness comments:

> If "evolution is good," then evolution must be allowed to proceed and the very process of change becomes absolutized. Such a view can be seen in Julian Huxley's *Evolutionary Ethics* or in the writings of Teilhard de Chardin. But in ever more areas, science is reaching the point of "destructive returns"; and the attempt to use evolution as a basis for morals and ethics is a failure. If evolutionary progress is taken as an axiom, then the trend toward convergence (social and evolutionary "unanimization") becomes a value, as suggested by Teilhard de Chardin. But this militates against the value of individuality and can be used to support totalitarianism. Bertrand Russell was typical of a growing majority who admit that science can be no more than neutral and does not speak directly into the area of moral choice (Os Guiness, *The Dust of Death*, Downers Grove, IL: InterVarsity Press, 1973, pp. 15, 16).

Mankind

Assumptions five and six of *Manifesto II* concern the nature of man, mankind. This is one of the most popular features of secular humanism, which is itself a form of the word human and so stresses continually the place of mankind in its philosophy.

> Fifth: The preciousness and dignity of the individual person is a central humanist value. Individuals should be encouraged to realize their own creative talents and desires. We reject all religious, ideological, or moral codes that denigrate the individual, suppress freedom, dull intellect, dehumanize personality. We believe in maximum individual autonomy con-

sonant with social responsibility. Although science can account for the causes of behavior, the possibilities of individual *freedom of choice* exist in human life and should be increased.

Sixth: In the area of sexuality, we believe that intolerant attitudes, often cultivated by orthodox religions and puritanical cultures, unduly repress sexual conduct. The right to birth control, abortion, and divorce should be recognized. While we do not approve of exploitive, denigrating forms of sexual expression, neither do we wish to prohibit, by law or social sanction, sexual behavior between consenting adults. The many varieties of sexual exploration should not in themselves be considered "evil." Without countenancing mindless permissiveness or unbridled promiscuity, a civilized society should be a *tolerant* one. Short of harming others or compelling them to do likewise, individuals should be permitted to express the sexual proclivities and pursue their life-styles as they desire. We wish to cultivate the development of a responsible attitude toward sexuality, in which humans are not exploited as sexual objects, and in which intimacy, sensitivity, respect, and honesty in interpersonal relations are encouraged. Moral education for children and adults is an important way of developing awareness and sexual maturity.

The secular humanist position on relative moral values is almost the watershed for critiquing humanistic tenets. With no absolute ethic, why should we accept the humanists' moral value that the individual person is precious and deserves dignity in his own right? The Marxist, for example, argues that the individual only has worth as a member of society. It is permissible, indeed necessary, to expend the individual for the society. Why isn't the Marxist right? How can the humanist infringe on the Marxist's individual preciousness and dignity by telling him his view of mankind is wrong?

The term "social responsibility" is an empty one since each society differs in what it considers responsible behavior. The rule of the society can change at any moment.

Furthermore, is there objective evidence for this unmitigated optimism concerning man's ability to direct his own development and fulfillment? Os Guiness points out that many don't think so:

A persistent erosion of man's view of himself is occurring. The fact that man has made so many significant scientific discoveries points strongly to the significance of man, yet the

> content of these same scientific discoveries underscores his insignificance. Man finds himself dwarfed bodily by the vast stretches of space and belittled temporally by the long reaches of time. Humanists are caught in a strange dilemma. If they affirm the greatness of man, it is only at the expense of ignoring his aberrations. If they regard human aberrations seriously, they have to escape the dilemma raised, either by blaming the situation on God (and how often those most strongly affirming the non-existence of God have a perverse propensity to question his goodness!) or by reducing man to the point of insignificance where his aberrations are no longer a problem. During World War II, Einstein, plagued by the mounting monstrosity of man against man, was heard to mutter to himself, "After all, this is a small star." He escaped the dilemmas of man's crime and evil but only at a price of undermining man's significance. A supreme characteristic of men today is the high degree of dissatisfaction with their own views of themselves. The opposition to determinism is growing not because determinism explains nothing but because it explains too much. It is a clutching constriction on that which man feels himself to be. Arthur Koestler attacks it as "ratomorphic," Vicktor Frankl as "modern nihilism" and Norman Chomsky as "the flat earth view of man."
>
> Mortimer Adler's *The Difference of Man and the Difference It Makes* is one book which probes deeply in this area and is scrupulously objective in its extensive analysis. He warns that if man continues to recognize no fundamental difference in kind between himself and the world of animals and machines, then his view of himself in terms of his moral dilemma or his metaphysical being must alter irretrievably. Anything left of contemporary concepts of morality and identity will be reduced to the level of the illusory, and the implications for individuals and for civilization are far-reaching (ibid., pp. 16, 17).

Humanist Manifesto II has a contradictory statement about human sexuality. While championing the autonomy of individual sexual rights, the statement also contradictorily makes bold universal moral assertions about some kinds of sex. What right do the humanist signers of this *Manifesto* have to say they do not approve of "exploitive, denigrating forms of sexual expression" or "mindless permissiveness or unbridled promiscuity"? What if an individual *likes* such sexual activity? If the humanists were to reply that such activity denies the rights of other parties, we must ask, what right have the humanists to say that those others' rights should come before the particular individual's rights?

In short, without an absolute standard of ethics by which one's sexual attitudes are determined, one cannot successfully argue for the universal adoption of his own subjective ethics. The secular humanists may have decided among themselves that certain forms of sexual behavior are "wrong," but they have no right to enforce their ideas on anyone who disagrees.

As Christians we believe that God is the source of our ethical system. Because He commands us to have respect and love for others, it is therefore wrong to engage in exploitive and denigrating forms of sexual expression. A Christian's sexual ethics should follow from God's character, expressed to man.

The Bible also strongly disagrees with any taking of human life, even if such murder is disguised with the empty word "abortion." Doesn't abortion exploit and denigrate the unborn child who is its victim?

Society

Articles seven through eleven of *Humanist Manifesto II* deal with the secular humanist view of and hope for society. These articles touch on politics, sociology, and economics.

> Seventh: To enhance freedom and dignity the individual must experience a full range of civil liberties in all societies. This includes freedom of speech and the press, political democracy, the legal right of opposition to governmental policies, fair judicial process, religious liberty, freedom of association, and artistic, scientific, and cultural freedom. It also includes a recognition of an individual's right to die with dignity, euthanasia, and the right to suicide. We oppose the increasing invasion of privacy, by whatever means, in both totalitarian and democratic societies. We would safeguard, extend, and implement the principles of human freedom evolved from the Magna Charta to the Bill of Rights, the Rights of Man, and the Universal Declaration of Human Rights.
>
> Eighth: We are committed to an open and democratic society. We must extend participatory democracy in its true sense to the economy, the school, the family, the workplace, and voluntary associations. Decision-making must be decentralized to include widespread involvement of people at all levels—social, political, and economic. All persons should have a voice in developing the values and goals that determine their lives. Institutions should be responsive to expressed desires and

needs. The conditions of work, education, devotion, and play should be humanized. Alienating forces should be modified or eradicated and bureaucratic structures should be held to a minimum. People are more important than decalogues, rules, proscriptions, or regulations.

Ninth: The separation of church and state and the separation of ideology and state are imperatives. The state should encourage maximum freedom for different moral, political, religious, and social values in society. It should not favor any particular religious bodies through the use of public monies, nor espouse a single ideology and function thereby as an instrument of propaganda or oppression, particularly against dissenters.

Tenth: Human societies should evaluate economic systems not by rhetoric or ideology, but by whether or not they increase economic well-being for all individuals and groups, minimize poverty and hardship, increase the sum of human satisfaction, and enhance the quality of life. Hence the door is open to alternative economic systems. We need to democratize the economy and judge it by its responsiveness to human needs, testing results in terms of the common good.

Eleventh: The principle of moral equality must be furthered through elimination of all discrimination based upon race, religion, sex, age, or national origin. This means equality of opportunity and recognition of talent and merit. Individuals should be encouraged to contribute to their own betterment. If unable, then society should provide means to satisfy their basic economic, health, and cultural needs, including, wherever resources make possible, a minimum guaranteed annual income. We are concerned for the welfare of the aged, the infirm, the disadvantaged, and also for the outcasts—the mentally retarded, abandoned or abused children, the handicapped, prisoners, and addicts—for all who are neglected or ignored by society. Practicing humanists should make it their vocation to humanize personal relations. . . .

We deplore racial, religious, ethnic, or class antagonisms. Although we believe in cultural diversity and encourage racial and ethnic pride, we reject separations which promote alienation and set people and groups against each other; we envision an integrated community where people have a maximum opportunity for free and voluntary association.

We are critical of sexism or sexual chauvinism—male or female. We believe in equal rights for both women and men to fulfill their unique careers and potentialities as they see fit, free of invidious discrimination.

Rather than picking these articles apart piece by piece,

we will offer some general observations in criticism. Our two major criticisms go back to two of the most basic presuppositions of secular humanism: relative morals and the basic goodness of mankind.

Because the secular humanists state that all ethics/morals/values are subjective and situational, they cannot support their system consistently and yet retain absolute values. However, many statements in these five articles do assume absolute values. We are told (article seven) that the individual "must experience a full range of civil liberties" to "enhance freedom and dignity." What's so great about freedom and dignity? Why should we accept the humanists' dogmatic assertion that human freedom and dignity are values all men should strive for? We are told that the individual has the "right to die with dignity, euthanasia, and the right to suicide." How can relativistic secular humanists make such a value judgment? Why have the secular humanists decided that it is universally wrong to kill someone else (murder), but it is morally right to choose to kill yourself (suicide)?

As Christians we are not asked, nor do we ask others, to support an arbitrary, finite system of absolute values just on the basis of our having proposed it. We believe that there are absolute values and morals because God, the framer and sustainer of this world, has designed the world to work in accordance with His intrinsic attributes of goodness, love, etc., and to malfunction (as in the fall) when its members do not harmonize with God's will.

As Christians we are dedicated to the freedom of man as an individual because God demonstrated the importance of that freedom in the freedom he gave man, a freedom that includes rejecting man's very Maker and his provision of peace and eternal joy. As Christians we believe that life is sacred because it is a gift from God, its origin and sustainer. It is not for man to decide the time of death, for another person or for himself. Christianity has an absolute standard of values based on the Creator of all things.

Secular humanism and Christianity are diametrically opposed on the moral bent of mankind. Secular humanism assumes that everyone is basically good (with a few exceptions) and that evil comes from outside people and societies, rather than from within. This is somewhat like the naive view of Marxism, which taught that if the evils of society were only eradicated, evil men would cease to exist.

While Christians should applaud secular humanism's commitment to racial, social, and sexual integration, we should not lose sight of the fact that removing the trappings of bigotry does not remove the evil seeds of that bigotry from within the individual. Society will never be transformed by tampering with the mechanics of social intercourse. Neither will it be reshaped into Utopia by temporarily forcing evil men to act like good men. The only way to change society is to transform the individuals within that society.

Christianity teaches that all of mankind made its choice for evil in the person of Adam at the fall. The Bible says that man is not basically good, but basically bad (see Romans 3:10, 23, 30; 6:23). Only through the freewill appropriation of the atoning work of Jesus Christ on the cross can a man be turned from evil to good. The Christian works to transform the individuals who compose society. This alone will bring about true change in the society.

One-World Government

Many people in Western society are turning toward the idea of a one-world government as the solution to the problems of mankind. This idea does not belong to the secular humanists alone. A great number of those who are oriented toward Eastern philosophy and religion believe that world unity will be accomplished only in this way. In fact, the Bible itself teaches that God eventually will establish a one-world government. However, under discussion here is the secular humanist view of a one-world system, as described in *Manifesto II*, articles twelve, thirteen, fourteen and fifteen.

> Twelfth: We deplore the division of humankind on nationalistic grounds. We have reached a turning point in human history where the best option is to transcend the limits of national sovereignty and to move toward the building of a world community in which all sectors of the human family can participate. Thus we look to the development of a system of world law and a world order based upon transnational federal government. This would appreciate cultural pluralism and diversity. It would not exclude pride in national origins and accomplishments nor the handling of regional problems on a regional basis. Human progress, however, can no longer be

achieved by focusing on one section of the world, Western or Eastern, developed or underdeveloped. For the first time in human history, no part of humankind can be isolated from any other. Each person's future is in some way linked to all. We thus reaffirm a commitment to the building of world community, at the same time recognizing that this commits us to some hard choices.

Thirteenth: This world community must renounce the resort to violence and force as a method of solving international disputes. We believe in the peaceful adjudication of differences by international courts and by the development of the arts of negotiation and compromise. War is obsolete. So is the use of nuclear, biological, and chemical weapons. It is a planetary imperative to reduce the level of military expenditures and turn these savings to peaceful and people-oriented uses.

Fourteenth: The world community must engage in cooperative planning concerning the use of rapidly depleting resources. The planet earth must be considered a single ecosystem. Ecological damage, resource depletion, and excessive population growth must be checked by international concord. The cultivation and conservation of nature is a moral value, we should perceive ourselves as integral to the sources of our being in nature. We must free our world from needless pollution and waste, responsibly guarding and creating wealth, both natural and human. Exploitation of natural resources, uncurbed by social conscience, must end.

Fifteenth: The problems of economic growth and development can no longer be resolved by one nation alone; they are worldwide in scope. It is the moral obligation of the developed nations to provide—through an international authority that safeguards human rights—massive technical, agricultural, medical, and economic assistance, including birth control techniques, to the developing portions of the globe. World poverty must cease. Hence extreme disproportions in wealth, income, and economic growth should be reduced on a worldwide basis.

We believe that men live by absolute ethics even if they claim to believe only in relative ethics. One may say that all ethics and moral values are relative to one's society or to the individual conviction, but one rarely lives by such a maxim. This we find with the secular humanists who drafted *Humanist Manifesto II*.

The beginning of *Manifesto II* declares that morals and values are relative and largely governed by society. Yet in these four articles we find such absolute moral values as "the best option is to transcend the limits of national sovereignty," belief in "peaceful adjudication of differences by international courts and by the development of the arts of negotiation and compromise," "the cultivation and conservation of nature is a moral value," and "it is the moral obligation of the developed nations to provide...massive...assistance,...to the developing portions of the globe."

Christians would not necessarily disagree with the above moral values. But Christians have an absolute ground for their ethics. Christian morality does not depend on the shifting subjective standards of any particular society or vocal group of people. Biblical Christianity depends on the Sovereign of the universe for its moral values.

In the twelfth article the humanists say that adopting a one-world government would commit us to "some hard choices." Unfortunately for the layman, those choices are not identified. We would worry that, in their zeal to establish Utopia, secular humanists might consider it a hard but necessary choice to sacrifice certain dissident individuals for the better choice of promoting the one-world Utopian government. Isn't this just the sort of "choice" we Westerners decry as human rights violations in many Marxist countries today? (See the chapter on Marxism for a discussion of the role—or lack of role— of the individual in the struggle for the classless society.) The Christian cannot endorse article twelve without knowing just what "hard choices" face the one-world government advocate.

According to God's Word, just before the second coming of Jesus Christ to establish His kingdom, the forces of Satan will attempt to set up a one-world system, implementing worship and submission to Satan's representative, the Anti-Christ. (See Matthew 24, 1 and 2 Thessalonians and the book of Revelation.) The secular humanists, at least in that day, will get their wish of a one-world government. But it will not usher in Utopia, rather it will bring on Armageddon.

As we discussed previously, the secular humanists diverge sharply from the Christian perspective by assuming that mankind is basically good. Many of the goals of a one-world government are lofty and not in oppostion to Christianity. However, the feasibility of implementing such changes is almost non-existent given the biblical presupposition that man is basically bad instead of good.

It sounds good to say that the "world community must renounce the resort to violence and force" and that "war is obsolete." However, a proclamation by itself never altered reality. Just how do the secular humanists propose to guarantee that everyone in a position of power will give up the use of force? And if even one person with power chooses to use it to force his own views, what will the humanist recourse be? Will he sweet-talk the offender? Or use force to teach him not to use force?

Christianity does not advocate the use of force to spread one's values and beliefs. However, Christianity recognizes that self-centered men will use force. Christianity sees the ultimate "weapon" against force as being an individual whose life has been transformed by the power of the Holy Spirit and whose will has been surrendered to the Lord Jesus Christ. Only when men are changed will violence cease. The Bible tells us the time will come when there will be no more violence. Such a world will not come about by proclamation of secular humanism, but by the divine command, judgment and forgiveness of the Lord (Revelation 20, 21).

In the meantime, the Bible specifically places responsibility for self-defense on the individual. We have a God-given obligation to protect those who depend on us. We must ensure the safety of our families. Christians may disagree about what sort of resistance is meant in the Bible. Whether or not a Christian allows for the use of force to safeguard those for whom he is responsible, he understands the serious charge God has given him and recognizes through it the measure of the value God places on each human life.

The use of abortion appears to be allowed by both articles fourteen and fifteen of *Manifesto II*. Article fourteen states that "excessive population growth must be checked" and article fifteen calls birth control techniques a "human right." Taken with the previous *Manifesto II* statement in article six regarding abortion as a human right, we can see that it is very likely that the secular humanists, if given the chance, would solve population booms with, among other things, abortions. We repeat what we said earlier: does it contribute to the dignity and value of the individual human life to murder it if it is inconvenient, if it doesn't fit into the world plan for conservation of resources and if it just happens not to have been born yet? Christians cannot agree to taking innocent human life in the name of any world plan.

Article fifteen presents a socialistic world economy as the only society of value. How is this new society to be obtained? It is easy to say "disproportions in wealth, income, and economic growth should be reduced on a worldwide basis." But how is this to be accomplished? Do the secular humanists actually think it likely that the wealthy of this world will, en masse and without exception, give up their wealth and distribute it to the poor? If so, why hasn't it already happened? If mankind is basically good, society should need no impetus such as a *Humanist Manifesto II* for the wealthy to share with the poor.

Perhaps the secular humanists are not so naive as that. What then, is their solution? Should they use force to relieve the rich of their "economic burdens" and then bless the poor with the wealth taken from the rich? It seems the humanists will break either article thirteen banning violence or article fifteen banning private wealth. Marxism and socialism have similar economic goals. A look at the "freedom" of contemporary Marxist and Socialist societies show us that these goals are not realistic.

Science

The last two propositions by the secular humanists offer the tools for implementing the grand scheme: science and its workhorse, technology. Somewhere in science, they say, lies the solution to the problems of mankind.

> Sixteenth: Technology is a vital key to human progress and development. We deplore any neo-romantic efforts to condemn indiscriminately all technology and science or to counsel retreat from its further extension and use for the good of humankind. We would resist any moves to censor basic scientific research on moral, political, or social grounds. Technology must, however, be carefully judged by the consequences of its use; harmful and destructive changes should be avoided. We are particularly disturbed when technology and bureaucracy control, manipulate, or modify human beings without their consent. Technological feasibility does not imply social or cultural desirability.

> Seventeenth: We must expand communication and transportation across frontiers. Travel restrictions must cease. The world must be open to diverse political, ideological, and moral viewpoints and evolve a worldwide system of television and radio for information and education. We thus call for full international cooperation in culture, science, the arts and technology, across ideological borders. We must learn to live openly together or we shall perish together.

When all else is said, it appears that the humanists rely on science and its evolution to provide the magic formulas needed to materialize the new world order envisioned by the humanists. Christianity is not intrinsically antagonistic to science. In fact, it is the Christian God who created the world around us and who determined its laws and functions, which have been categorized by what we call science. Colossians 1:16-17 reminds us that it is to the Lord Jesus Christ that we owe our existence:

> For in Him all things were created, both in the heavens and on earth, visible and invisible, whether thrones or dominions or rulers or authorities—all things have been created through Him and for Him. And He is before all things, and in Him all things hold together (NASB).

Science does not create laws of nature, it discovers them. When science does discover one of those laws,it is no surprise to God. However, science is no substitute for God. All science can do is discover and describe, it cannot create reality *ex nihilo* (out of nothing).

While we would not dismiss out of hand any particular advance of science, we would question the humanists' assertion that all science will be used "for the good of humankind" and that "carefully judged by the consequences of its use; harmful and destructive changes should be avoided." We return to the same but still valid critique: who is to determine what the "good of humankind" is, and who is to enforce the judgments of whomever has been chosen to determine that good? The spectre of George Orwell's *1984* looms threateningly as we think of the abuses, intentional or not, to which such judgment and enforcement could be put.

Finally, we agree with the last sentence of proposition seventeen: "We must learn to live openly together or we shall perish together." This is exactly what the Bible has to say. However, the Bible states that because man is basically self-centered and sinful, he will forever be unable to live peaceably with his fellow man on his own initiative. It takes the supernatural intervention of God to transform individuals into selfless, caring, loving people who really will sacrifice their own desires for the sake of their fellow men. Universal peace will come only with the intervention of Almighty God. We see expressed in 2 Peter 3:3-14 the biblical vision of the future, a future cleansed of evil by judgment and restored in love by the Lord Jesus Christ:

> Know this first of all, that in the last days mockers will come with their mocking, following after their own lusts, and saying, 'Where is the promise of His coming? For ever since the fathers fell asleep, all continues just as it was from the beginning of creation.' For when they maintain this, it escapes their notice that by the word of God the heavens existed long ago and the earth was formed out of water and by water, through which the world at that time was destroyed, being flooded with water. But the present heavens and earth by His word are being reserved for fire, kept for the day of judgment and destruction of ungodly men. But do not let this one fact escape your notice, beloved, that with the Lord one day is as a thousand years, and a thousand years as one day. The Lord is not slow about His promise, as some count slowness, but is patient toward you, not wishing for any to perish but for all to come to repentance. But the day of the Lord will come like a thief, in which the heavens will pass away with a roar and the elements will be destroyed with intense heat, and the earth and its works will be burned up. Since all these things are to be destroyed in this way, what sort of people ought you to be in holy conduct and godliness, looking for and hastening the coming of the day of God, on account of which the heavens will be destroyed by burning, and the elements will melt with intense heat! But according to His promise we are looking for new heavens and a new earth, in which righteousness dwells. Therefore, beloved, since you look for these things, be diligent to be found by Him in peace, spotless and blameless (NASB).

Humanism Bibliography

Angeles, Peter A., Dictionary of Philosophy. NY: Harper and Row, Publishers, 1981.

Edwards, Rem. B., *Reason and Religion*. NY: Harcourt Brace Jovanovich, Inc., 1972.

Flew, Antony, *A Dictionary of Philosophy*. NY: St. Martin's Press, 1982.

Geisler, Norman, *Is Man the Measure: An Evaluation of Contemporary Humanism*. Grand Rapids, MI: Baker Book House, 1982.

Green, Michael, *Man Alive*. Downers Grove, IL: InterVarsity Press, 1968.

Guiness, Os, *The Dust of Death*. Downers Grove, IL: InterVarsity Press, 1973.

Horvath, Nicholas A., *Philosophy*. Woodbury, NY: Barron's Educational Series, 1974.

Kurtz, Paul W., *The Humanist Alternative*. London: Pemberton Press, 1973.

———— ed., *Humanist Manifesto I and II*. Buffalo, NY: Prometheus Books, 1973.

Lamont, Corliss, *Freedom of Choice Affirmed*. NY: New Horizon Publishers, 1967.

————, *The Independent Mind*. NY: New Horizon Publishers, 1951.

Maritain, Jacques, *True Humanism*. Westport, CT: Greenwood Press, 1970.

Pascal, Blaise, *Pense's No. 430*. Trans. H. F. Stewart, NY: Random House, n.d.

Purtill, Richard, *C. S. Lewis's Case for the Christian Faith*. San Francisco: Harper and Row, Publishers, 1981.

Runes, Dagobert D., ed., *Dictionary of Philosophy*. Totowa, NJ: Littlefield, Adams and Company, 1977.

Sahakian, William S., *History of Philosophy*. NY: Harper and Row, Publishers, 1968.

————, and Mabel L. Sahakian, *Ideas of the Great Philosophers*. NY: Harper and Row, Publishers, 1966.

Schaeffer, Francis, *Death in the City*. Downers Grove, IL: InterVarsity Press, 1969.

Sire, James, *The Universe Next Door*. Downers Grove, IL: InterVarsity Press, 1976.

Stumpf, Samuel Enoch, *Socrates to Sartre: A History of Philosophy*. NY: McGraw-Hill Book Company, 1966.

Young, Warren C., *A Christian Approach to Philosophy*. Grand Rapids, MI: Baker Book House, 1954.

CHAPTER FOUR

Existentialism

Existentialism, a difficult system to define, has been developing over the last fifty years. As it evolved it attracted followers from many different backgrounds. Today its influence has subtly affected much popular thought and expression. As F. H. Heinemann observes

> Among contemporary philosophies none has made a greater impact on religion and theology than existentialism (F. H. Heinemann, *Existentialism and the Modern Predicament*, NY: Harper and Row, Publishers, 1953, p. 219).

Because of its pervasive influence and incompatibility with orthodox Christianity, existentialism should be answered in a Christian response to secular religion.

The Difficulty of Definition

One of existentialism's problems is that it is difficult to define or categorize concisely. Philosopher Walter Kaufmann comments:

> Existentialism is not a philosophy but a label for several widely different revolts against traditional philosophy. Most of the living "existentialists" have repudiated this label, and a bewildered outsider might well conclude that the only thing they have in common is a marked aversion for each other. To add to the confusion, many writers of the past have frequently been hailed as members of this movement, and it is extremely doubtful whether they would have appreciated the company to which they are consigned. In view of this, it might be argued

that the label "existentialism" ought to be abandoned altogether.

Certainly, existentialism is not a school of thought nor reducible to any set of tenets. The three writers who appear invariably on every list of "existentialists"—Jaspers, Heidegger, and Sartre—are not in agreement on essentials. Such alleged precursors as Pascal and Kierkegaard differed from all three men by being dedicated Christians; and Pascal was a Catholic of sorts while Kierkegaard was a Protestant's Protestant. If, as is often done, Nietzsche and Dostoevsky are included in the fold, we must make room for an impassioned anti-Christian and an even more fanatical Greek-Orthodox Russian imperialist. By the time we consider adding Rilke, Kafka, and Camus, it becomes plain that one essential feature shared by all these men is their perfervid individualism.

The refusal to belong to any school of thought, the repudiation of the adequacy of any body of beliefs whatever, and especially of systems, and a marked dissatisfaction with traditional philosophy as superficial, academic, and remote from life—that is the heart of existentialism (Walter Kaufmann, *Existentialism from Dostoevsky to Sartre*, NY: The World Publishing Company, 1956, pp. 11, 12).

Others echo Kaufmann's sentiment:

Every existentialist develops his own terminology because he finds everyday language inadequate, in the same way he rebels against a day-to-day view of the world. . . . if one reads the existentialists without exasperation, one is almost certainly misreading them (I. M. Bochenski, *Contemporary European Philosophy*, Berkeley and Los Angeles: University of California Press, 1956, p. 154, note 5).

Bochenski goes on to say:

. . . existentialism must not be identified with any one body of existentialist doctrine, for example, that of Sartre, for as we shall see there are profound differences between individual points of view (ibid., p. 156).

Existentialism Defined

Existentialism may be explained according to the themes and concerns of its proponents. Existentialists are concerned with existence, change, freedom and self-cognizance, among other things. William and Mabel Sahakian describe existentialism in the following manner:

Existentialists accept the conclusion that "existence precedes essence," and some go even further and affirm that essence does

> not exist, that only existence has reality. All Existentialists emphasize the person as subject. The subject exists, and for some, he alone exists; that is to say, if any essence whatever exists, it is the individual's subjective state of existence (William S. Sahakian and Mabel L. Sahakian, *Ideas of the Great Philosophers*, NY: Barnes and Noble, Inc., 1966, p. 167).

Philosopher B. A. G. Fuller recognizes the problems in defining existentialism, but also recognizes certain existential theses:

> There is no single existentialist position. The philosophy varies with its proponents, some of whom insist that they are not existentialists at all. But there is a common fund of doctrine that identifies them, nevertheless, and indicates quite clearly their relation to the classical philosophic tradition. Their major and differentiating thesis is the metaphysical pronouncement that "existence is prior to essence," while in the established tradition "essence is prior to existence." What this means for the existentialist is that human nature is determined by the course of life rather than life by human nature (B. A. G. Fuller, *A History of Philosophy*, NY: Holt, Rinehart and Winston, 1955, p. 603).

I. M. Bochenski, in his book *European Philosophy* relates six of the common existential themes:

> 1) The commonest characteristic among the various existentialist philosophies of the present is the fact that they all arise from a so-called existential *experience* which assumes a different form in each one of them. It is found by Jaspers, for instance, in awareness of the brittleness of being, by Heidegger through experiencing "propulsion toward death," and by Sartre in a general "nausea." The existentialists do not conceal the fact that their philosophies originate in such experiences. That is why existentialist philosophy always bears the stamp of personal experience, even in Heidegger.
>
> 2) The existentialists take so-called existence as the supreme object of inquiry, but the meaning which they attach to the word is extremely difficult to determine. However, in each case it signifies a peculiarly human mode of being. Man—a term which is rarely used and is generally replaced by "thereness" (Dasein), "existence," "ego," "being for oneself"—is unique in possessing existence; more precisely, man does not *possess*, but he *is* his existence. If man has an essence, either this essence is his existence or it is the consequence of it.
>
> 3) Existence is conceived as absolutely *actualistic*; it never *is* but freely *creates* itself, it becomes; it is a pro-jection; with each instant it is more (and less) than it is. The existentialists

> often support this thesis by the statement that existence is the same as temporality.
>
> 4) The difference between this actualism and that of life-philosophy is accounted for by the existentialists' regarding man as pure *subjectivity* and not as the manifestation of a broader (cosmic) life process in the way that Bergson does, for example. Furthermore, subjectivity is understood in a *creative* sense; man creates himself freely, and *is* his freedom.
>
> 5) Yet it would be thoroughly misguided to conclude from this that the existentialists regard man as shut up within himself. On the contrary, man is an incomplete and open reality; thus his nature pins him tightly and necessarily to the *world*, and to other men in particular. This double dependence is assumed by all representatives of existentialism, and in such a way that human existence seems to be inserted into the world, so that man at all times not only faces a determinate situation but *is* his situation. On the other hand they assume that there is a special connection between men which, like the situation, gives existence its peculiar quality. That is the meaning of Heidegger's "togetherness," Jasper's "communication," and Marcel's "thou."
>
> 6) All existentialists repudiate the distinction between subject and object, thereby discounting the value of *intellectual knowledge* for philosophical purposes. According to them true knowledge is not achieved by the understanding but through experiencing reality; this experience is primarily caused by the dread with which man becomes aware of his finitude and the frailty in that position of being thrust into the world and condemned to death [Heidegger] (Bochenski, *European Philosophy*, pp. 159, 160).

To summarize Bochenski, he identifies six major themes of existentialism: 1) experience as the ground of discovery; 2) existence as the supreme object of inquiry; 3) existence preceding essence; 4) man as pure subjectivity and not part of a cosmic life process; 5) the interdependence of man and his world; and 6) a devaluation of intellectual knowledge.

Finally, we will turn to philosopher Samuel Stumpf for his recognition of the fact that existentialists reject traditional philosophy:

> Whether they were theists or atheists, the existentialists all agreed that traditional philosophy was too academic and remote from life to have any adequate meaning for them. They rejected systematic and schematic thought in favor of a more spontaneous mode of expression in order to capture the authentic concerns of concrete existing individuals. Although there is no

"system" of existentialist philosophy, its basic themes can, nevertheless, be discovered in some representative existentialist thinkers (Samuel Enoch Stumpf, *Socrates to Sartre*, NY: McGraw-Hill, 1966, p. 455).

The Scope of Our Study

Our aim is to simplify an admittedly complex subject. Because of the intricate and sometimes contradictory assertions made among existentialists, we have decided to examine the themes of their reasoning as described by six leading philosophers often cited as shapers of existentialist thought. This method of treating the subject will avoid the sweeping and often erroneous generalizations made about this school of thought, but may result in some oversimplification.

Existentialism is more far-reaching than these six representative writers indicate. Moreover, some of these individuals would repudiate the label existentialist, finding it stultifying, although they deal with the same general themes from some of the same perspectives. We conclude with a Christian perspective on the thematic presuppositions of existentialism.

Religious Existentialists

Many Christians have never studied philosophy formally and are unfamiliar with the mainstream of existentialist thought. However, they have heard of a stream of existential thought that appears to be paradoxical. It is known as religious or Christian existentialism. Many Christians have at least a vague familiarity with some of the ideas of Karl Barth, Paul Tillich, and Rudolph Bultmann. We will not argue whether or not one can be religious and an existentialist at the same time. There are competent observers on both sides of the question. Almost every knowledgable observer, from either side, will agree that religious existentialism is not the same as orthodox existentialism. Even the term "orthodox existentialism" is a problem since the field is so diverse and the prominent existential thinkers don't agree about what existentialism is. Nevertheless, religious existentialists are concerned with some of the same themes as are non-religious existentialists. They just address them from different (religious) perspectives.

The Sahakians separate these two types of existentialists in much the same way as we will. They write:

> Two main schools of Existentialist philosophy may be distinguished; the first is religious as delineated by the father of Existentialism, Soren Aabye Kierkegaard (1813-1855); the second is atheistic, as expounded by its most articulate contemporary spokesman, Jean-Paul Sartre. A number of outstanding Existentialists in each of these schools disclaim the Existentialist label; some adherents of the religious view prefer to be known as Neo-Orthodox philosophers (Sahakian and Sahakian, *Ideas*, p. 167).

Fuller confirms this view, expanding on the perspectives of the religious existentialists:

> In its theistic form, existentialism has been an important factor in the neo-orthodox awakening that has marked theology since the first war. Its emphasis on the negative qualities of man, on human estrangement and the tragedy of human existence, have supported the resurgence of the dogma of original sin and the entire structure of eschatological theology (Fuller, *Philosophy*, pp. 603, 604).

Christian philosopher Milton Hunnex reveals how existentialism has penetrated modern theological circles:

> Unable to assimilate either the naturalism of Aristotle or that of the scientific revolution, Protestant theology eventually turned to idealism as the modern philosophy best adapted to Christian belief. Modern liberalism made its home among the idealists during the nineteenth century. After World War I it became apparent that idealism was ill suited to the twentieth century, and theologians as well as philosophers abandoned it. They turned instead to existentialism as the kind of philosophy that did appear to fit the mood and needs of the twentieth century. Existentialism seemed to be the best philosophy for getting at the problems of men caught up in swift-moving change (Milton D. Hunnex, *Existentialism and Christian Belief*, Chicago: Moody Press, 1969, pp. 13, 14).

Although we have chosen to examine this religious existentialist view of the controversy, we recognize that there are those who see no compromise between existentialism and religious belief. While we believe that they make some valid points, we feel the claims of the so-called religious existentialists still need to be dealt with, even if they do arise from a misunderstanding of existentialism and religion. Hazel Barnes recognizes the two sides of the controversy:

> I confess that I sympathize with the fundamentalist ministers who argue that whatever else it may be, this new religion is not Christianity and should be given some other name. (Hazel Barnes, *An Existentialist Ethics*, Chicago, IL: University of Chicago Press, 1978, p. 383).

We agree that historic Christianity cannot embrace the presuppositions and core of existentialist concern. However, there is much that claims the name "Christian" today that is not truly Christian in the biblical sense, but that must be dealt with by the biblically-centered Christian. We agree with Hazel Barnes that Sartrean existentialism (atheistic) cannot ever be reconciled with any form of theistic belief. She comments:

> I do not believe that religious existentialism is compatible with a position based on Sartrean premises. I do not find in Tillich's Being-itself a concept which is logically tenable or a reality existentially meaningful. I cannot see that Heidegger's Being is a valid or more valuable alternative to Sartre's Being-in-itself (ibid., p. 382).

As a final qualification, we recognize the distinction between theologians or religious thinkers who have existential orientations (existential theologians) and a true *existential theology*, which, almost by definition, cannot exist. We conclude, with Heinemann, who draws the general conclusion, that:

> *Existentialist Theology does not exist.* But the question remains to be answered: Can it exist? I am afraid the answer must be: No. The principle of existence is a call, an appeal (Jaspers), or in Kantian terminology, a regulative principle. It appeals to people to care for their inner life, for their freedom, their true self, their authentic existence, for their neighbours and their predicament. It admonishes us never to forget in thought and action the primacy of human persons as ends in themselves. It is not a constitutive principle, it defends the person against the menace of any kind of system and cannot therefore itself be the basis of a system. Existential Theology does not and cannot exist, but *existential theologians* should exist, that is theologians whose chief interest does not lie in dogmatics and in the external observance of rituals, but in the souls of men, in their predicament and in the willingness to help them. *Ex-*

istential theologians have always existed (Heinemann, *Existialism*, p. 225).

With the above factors in mind, we will look at three "religious existentialists," Sren Kierkegaard, Paul Tillich, and Gabriel Marcel.

Sren Kierkegaard (1813-1855)

Sren Aabye Kierkegaard was born in Copenhagen, Denmark, and was raised in an unusual religious family. His father had a morose obsession that God had cursed and doomed him and his family. The young Sren spent his youth convinced that continual, almost debilitating, depression was his fate. Of his youth he wrote:

> From a child I was under the sway of a prodigious melancholy, the depth of which finds its only adequate measure in the equally prodigious dexterity I possessed of hiding it under an apparent gaiety and *joie de vivre*. So far back as I can barely remember, my one joy was that nobody could discover how unhappy I felt (Soren Kierkegaard, *The Point of View for My Work as An Author: A Report to History*, NY: Harper and Row, Publishers, 1962, p. 76).

When Kierkegarrd entered the University of Copenhagen in 1830, he bowed to the wishes of his father and studied theology. However, his first love was philosophy, in which he excelled. He began to believe that he was predestined or chosen to change people for the better through philosophy. Late in life he reflected on his life, which he saw as developing dialectically,* and traced the path made "by the hand of God":

> About my *vita ante acta* (i.e. from childhood until I became an author) I cannot expatiate here at any length, however remarkable, as it seems to me, was the way I was predisposed from my earliest childhood, and step by step through the whole development, to become exactly the sort of author I became....
>
> An observer will perceive how everything was set in motion and how dialectically: I had a thorn in the flesh, intellectual gifts (especially imagination and dialectic) and culture in superabundance, an enormous development as an observer, a Christian upbringing that was certainly very unusual, a dialectical relationship to Christianity which was peculiarly my own,

---

*See chapter on Marxism for a discussion of dialectics.

> and in addition to this I had from childhood a training in obedience, obedience absolute, and I was armed with an almost foolhardy faith that I was able to do anything. . . . Finally, in my own eyes I was a penitent. The impression this now makes upon me is as if there were a Power which from the first instant had been observant of this and said, as a fisherman says of a fish, Let it run awhile, it is not yet the moment to pull it in. And strangely enough there is something that reaches far back in my recollection, impossible as it is for me to say when I began this practice or why such a thing ever occurred to me: I prayed to God regularly, i.e. every day, that He would give me zeal and patience to perform the work He would assign me.
>
> Thus I became an author (ibid., pp. 76, 82, 83).

Even in his most despondent moments, Kierkegaard said, he still had faith in God. But although he believed God existed and controlled the universe, he also believed he was doomed to depression. Speaking of his early beliefs, cultivated by his despondent father, he wrote:

> What wonder then that there were times when Christianity appeared to me the most inhuman cruelty—although never, even when I was farthest from it, did I cease to revere it, with a firm determination that (especially if I did not myself make the choice of becoming a Christian) I would never initiate anyone into the difficulties which I knew and which, so far as I have read and heard, no one else has alluded to. But I have never definitely broken with Christianity nor renounced it. To attack it has never been my thought. No, from the time when there could be any question of the employment of my powers, I was firmly determined to employ them all to defend Christianity, or in any case to present it in its true form (ibid., pp. 76,77).

In 1836, on the brink of suicide, he experienced the first of several religious encounters. The power of this experience led him to develop a system of morals (ethics) by which he determined to live his life.

In 1838 he had another religious experience that turned him toward a greater Christian commitment. He was also engaged to be married, but broke it off, feeling that marriage would interfere with his "mission" in life.

In later life, Kierkegaard viewed his writings as representing the three phases of human commitment: the aesthetic, the ethical, and the religious. His works, he believed, were in one way autobiographical, showing his own dialectical growth through the three stages. In another way, his writings were prototypical of the life experience that should be sought by each human being. And in still a third way, portions of his writings were not meant to represent his viewpoints at all, but were meant to encourage the reader to expand his own thinking patterns, entertain new belief systems, and thus dialectically grow toward the ultimate religious commitment, where he would find true peace. Most of Kierkegaard's writings were published under pseudonyms as part of his technique to encourage new thought. In 1843 he published *Either/Or* which, as he described it, expressed "the fact that I had become thoroughly aware how impossible it would be for me to be religious only up to a certain point. Here is the place of *Eithor/Or*. It was a poetical catharsis, which does not, however, go farther than the "ethical" (ibid., p. 18). In 1844 he published *The Concept of Dread and Philosophical Fragments*; in 1845 *Stages of Life's Way*; in 1846 *Concluding Unscientific Postscript*; in 1848 *Anti-Climacus* and *Christian Discourses*; and *The Point of View* was published after his death. These are the major writings of Kierkegaard.

Kierkegaard's writings had only limited influence during his lifetime. However, they were translated into other languages, mostly after his death, and his influence became tremendous. Because of this great later influence and his concerns with the existential themes of existence and the "authenticated" man, he became known as "the Father of Existentialism." Remember though, that he consistently referred to himself as a religious and even Christian thinker and would definitely not have aligned himself with the atheistic existentialists such as Sartre had he been alive in the twentieth century. His faith did not conform to historical and biblical Christianity, but it was religious faith nonetheless.

Kierkegaard's Philosophy

William S. Sahakian has concisely summarized Kierkegaard's main tenets:

> The essence of Kierkegaard's philosophy can be seen in his doctrine that there are three stages of life experience: (1) aesthetic, (2) ethical, and (3) religious. These represent three attitudes toward life, three philosophies of life. Some of us progress from one stage to the next, while others never go beyond the first

stage. Kierkegaard sometimes fused the second and third stages, referring to them as the religio-ethical. The third stage is superior to the other two stages. All of them reflect man's attempt to win salvation, to gain satisfaction for life's greatest good, while it is still within reach. Kierkegaard discussed the three stages in a number of his writings, but he devoted a most famous work, *Either/Or*, to a detailed analysis of the first two stages (William S. Sahakian, *History of Philosophy*, NY: Barnes and Noble Company, Inc., 1968, p. 343).

I. The Aesthetic

The man in the first stage, the aesthetic, is looking for fulfillment from his outside activities and from within himself. He may seek romance, pleasure, or intellectual pursuits as means to satisfy himself. However, these activities are not enough. They are not ultimately satisfying. The man becomes bored with himself and his activities. This boredom turns to despair. If not checked, the despair ends in suicide.

II. The Ethical

What is the remedy for this aesthetic despair? Kierkegaard replied that commitment gives meaning to life. Commitment to some arbitrary absolute, and the ordering of one's life around that commitment, brings one out of the aesthetic stage and into the second or ethical stage. The person achieves selfhood through commitment. The individual becomes aware. His choices are made with passion and emotional commitment. The person now chooses and acts, thereby establishing his selfhood and integrity. He is a man of duty. This is the type of person described by psychotherapist Viktor Frankl, who revolutionized European psycho-analytic theory after World War II. He calls the ethical urge the "will to meaning" and says:

> Man's search for meaning is a primary force in his life and not a "secondary rationalization" of instinctual drives. This meaning is unique and specific in that it must and can be fulfilled by him alone; only then does it achieve a significance that will satisfy his own will to meaning. There are some authors who contend that meanings and values are "nothing but defense mechanisms, reaction formations and sublimation." But as for myself, I would not be willing to live merely for the sake of my "defense mechanisms," nor would I be ready to die merely for the sake of my "reaction formations." Man, however, is able

to live and even to die for the sake of his ideals and values! (Viktor E. Frankl, *Man's Search for Meaning: an Introduction to Logotherapy*, NY: Simon and Schuster, Inc., 1963, pp. 154, 155).

III. The Religious

The third and greatest stage, the stage where man finally finds contentment, is the religious stage. The person commits himself, as in the second stage, and is looking for fulfillment, as in the first stage, but in this religious stage his commitment is to One who is able to satisfy completely: God. In this stage man is finally content because of his commitment to God. Selfhood cannot be achieved ultimately and completely within the self. The self must be committed to the One beyond, to God.

Kierkegaard and Hegel

Kierkegaard's philosophy was in opposition to that of the German philosopher Hegel, although they both used a system of dialectics. Samuel Stumpf points out:

> At the University of Copenhagen Kierkegaard was trained in Hegel's philosophy and was not favorably impressed by it. When he heard Schellings's lectures at Berlin, which were critical of Hegel, Kierkegaard agreed with this attack upon Germany's greatest speculative thinker. "If Hegel had written the whole of his Logic and then said. . . that it was merely an experiment in thought," wrote Kierkegaard, "then he could certainly have been the greatest thinker who ever lived. As it is, he is merely comic." What made Hegel comic for Kierkegaard was that this great philosopher had tried to capture all of reality in his system of thought, yet in the process lost the most important element, namely, *existence*. For Kierkegaard, the term *existence* was reserved for the individual human being. To exist, he said, implies being a certain kind of individual, an individual who strives, who considers alternatives, who chooses, who decides, and who, above all, commits himself. Virtually none of these acts were implied in Hegel's philosophy (Stumpf, *Socrates*, p. 455).

William Sahakian made some good contrasts between the concerns of Hegel and the concerns of Kierkegaard:

> Kierkegaardian philosophy is fundamentally in direct antithesis to Hegelianism. Whereas Hegel placed the emphasis on speculative thought, Kierkegaard placed it on existence. Hegel

discerned truth in the rational system, Kierkegaard in paradox. The former sought the universe, the latter the individual or particular. The former saw in logic a mediation of anitheses or formulated an unbroken logic (Hegelian dialectic); the latter replaced it with the leap or logical gap (qualitative dialectic). *Either/Or* was the Kierkegaardian answer to the Hegelian synthesis or mediation. Hegel found truth in the Absolute and objectivity, while Kierkegaard found it in the relative and subjective. Hegel emphasized necessity, Kierkegaard freedom. Other Kierkegaardian concepts, which replaced Hegelian ones were: repetition for recollection, concealment for openness, possibility for actuality, indirect communication (Socratic maimetic) for direct communication, transcendence of God for the immanence of God, and mediacy (or reflection) or immediacy (Sahakian *Philosophy*, p. 347).

Kierkegaard and Truth

Kierkegaard defined truth as "subjectivity." For him it was paradoxically the only thing one could be sure about and yet the one thing one was anxious about. Sahakian explains:

> Truth is subjectivity; the highest expression of subjectivity is passion. To think Existentially is to think with inward passion. Objectivity accents *what* is said, but subjectivity accents *how* it is said. The inward *how* is passion; decision is found only in subjectivity. Subjectivity is the truth; truth is defined as "an objective uncertainty held fast in an appropriation-process of the most passionate inwardness." Uncertainty creates anxiety which is quieted by an exercise of faith. The preceding definition of truth also serves as a definition of faith. There is no faith without risk, choice, passion, and inwardness; nor is there truth without them. Uncertainty always accompanies subjectivity, calling for the leap of faith (ibid., p. 348).

The Christian philosophers Norman Geisler and Paul Feinberg point out a very important feature of Kierkegaardian "truth." They note that Kierkegaard never denies such a thing as *objective* truth: he merely denies its importance over what he calls *"subjective"* truth.

> While not denying that there is such a thing as *objective* scientific truth, the existentialist does not consider that kind of truth important, at least not nearly as important as *subjective* truth. Indeed, Kierkegaard declared "truth is subjectivity." By that he did not mean that any subjective belief is true, but that unless one believes something subjectively and passionately he does not possess the truth. Truth is always personal and not mere-

> ly propositional. One never gains truth by mere observation, but by obedience: never by being a spectator, but only by being a participator in life. Truth is found in the concrete, not in the abstract: in the existential, not in the rational. In fact, one places himself in the truth only by an act of his will, by a "leap of faith." It is not deliberation of the mind but a decision of the will by which one comes to know truth (Norman L. Geisler and Paul D. Feinberg, *Introduction to Philosophy*, Grand Rapids, MI: Baker Book House, 1980, p. 46).

In summary, Kierkegaardian philosophy is much more complicated than at first meets the eye. One especially must be aware that common and philosophical vocabularies take on new definitions for Kierkegaard. The evangelical Christian who declares that Jesus Christ is the truth means something quite different from what Kierkegaard means. KIerkegaard's three-fold path to personal fulfillment sounds good until it is examined from within the context of the claims of the Bible or until attempts are made to authenticate it by history and objective reason.

Paul Tillich (1886-1965)

One of the most influential liberal theologians of the twentieth century was Paul Tillich. Because of his orientation in both existentialist themes and Christian tradition, he rightly can be called an existential theologian. F. H. Heinemann notes:

> The title 'existentialist theologian' would fit. . . Paul Tillich. His unique case is that of a philosopher-theologian who started as a religious socialist and ends up as an existential theologian. Being a philosopher as well as a theologian, he tries to correlate philsophy and religion, embraces existentialism as the true philosophy whose task it is to penetrate the structure of human existence (Heinemann, *Existentialism*, p. 219).

Alston and Nakhnikian give some of Tillich's Lutheran, liberal theology, and philosophical background:

> Paul Tillich is one of the most influential Christian thinkers of our time—perhaps the most influential in English-speaking countries. Born in a small village in eastern Germany in 1886, the son of a Lutheran pastor, he received a theological and philosophical education, and was ordained in the Evangelical Lutheran Church in 1912. After serving as an army chaplain during World War I, Tillich taught theology and philosophy at several German universities—Berlin, Marburg, Dresden, and

Frankfurt. He incurred the wrath of the Nazis, and when Hitler came to power in 1933 he emigrated to the United States. On his arrival in America he became a Professor of theology at Union Theological Seminary. From this post Tillich has exercised an enormous influence on religious thought in this country. (William P. Alston and George Nakhnikian, *Readings in Twentieth Century Philosophy*, NY: The Free Press, 1963, p. 723).

Anxiety

Anxiety is one of the very important themes in existentialism. Although different existentialists handle the theme in different ways, Tillich's discussion of anxiety in his *Systematic Theology* gives a very thorough discussion of the subject from an existential point of view. Philosopher B. A. G. Fuller summarizes Tillich's discussion:

Anxiety. Accepting the familiar description of the post-war era, both for Europe and America, as an "age of anxiety," Tillich describes anxiety as fundamentally the "existential awareness of nonbeing," the "awareness that nonbeing is a part of one's own being." The awareness of one's own transitoriness and of one's own having to die produces a natural anxiety, an anxiety of ultimate nonbeing. Naked anxiety, which belongs to the nature of being as such and is an experience of unimaginable horror, strives vainly to convert itself into fear, because fear has an object and can therefore be met and overcome by courage. But anxiety itself has no object.

The Anxiety of Fate and Death. Anxiety appears in three forms, dependent upon the direction in which "nonbeing threatens being." The *anxiety of fate and death* proceeds from the threat of nonbeing against man's "ontic" affirmation. It is basic, universal, and entirely inescapable. The contingency of man, that the causes which determine him are without any rationality or ultimate necessity, yields the relative anxiety of fate. The fact of death, present with man during every moment of life as well as at the moment of dying, produces an absolute anxiety of nonbeing. The basic question of courage is whether there is a *courage to be* in the face of this absolute threat against being.

The Anxiety of Emptiness and Meaninglessness. The second type of anxiety is in its relative form the *anxiety of emptiness* and in its absolute form the *anxiety of meaninglessness.* Emptiness is the product of a threat to participation in creativity. Meaninglessness, which lies always in the background of emptiness as death lies always behind fate, is the loss of a spiritual center for life, the loss of an ultimate concern, of the meaning fundamental to all meanings. This anxiety is the threat of nonbeing to the spiritual life, a threat that follows from man's finitude and estrangement and leads to despair. To escape it, one attempts an escape from his own freedom and thereby sacrifices his genuine existence.

The Anxiety of Guilt and Condemnation. The third type of anxiety issues from the threat of nonbeing against man's self-affirmation, in its relative form, the *anxiety of guilt;* in its absolute form, the *anxiety of condemnation.* Man as finite freedom is free to determine himself in the fulfillment of his destiny. The anxiety of guilt and condemnation is produced by the failure to realize one's potentiality. It is a self-rejection, a despair in the loss of proper identity. Despair is the product of the three anxieties, interrelated to foster and support one another. Despair is the complete absence of hope. By suicide one might escape the anxiety of death, but he would be caught in the anxiety of guilt and condemnation.

Anxiety and Cultural History. Life, Tillich holds, is largely an attempt to avoid despair. From it there is no escape, yet most people experience it in its intensity only infrequently if at all. In the history of western culture the three types of anxiety have always been present, but each has dominated one of the three major eras. The classical era, the era of absolutism and tyranny, was characterized by the anxiety of fate and death, and ended with the attempt to achieve the Stoic courage. The Middle Ages, under the influence of the Judeo-Christian (Moral) religion, was brought to a close under the domination of the anxiety of guilt and condemnation, induced by the breakdown of the unity of religion. Today it is the anxiety of emptiness and meaninglessness that casts its shadow over a world that has lost its spiritual content. (B. A. G. Fuller, *Philosophy*, pp. 609-610).

God

Tillich's definition of God was much more broad than that of evangelical Christianity or the Bible. In fact, Tillich's concept of God was not even first and foremost personal. God for Tillich was "the ground of all being," "the source of your being," "your ultimate concern." As such, Tillich saw no room for atheists or agnostics, for he believed that it was impossible for one to have no ultimate concerns. In his *The Shaking of the Foundations* he stated:

> The name of this infinite and inexhaustible depth and ground of all being is *God*. That depth is what the word *God* means. And if that word has not much meaning for you, translate it,

> and speak of the depths of your life, of the source of your being, of your ultimate concern, of what you take seriously without any reservation. . . . If you know that God means depth, you know much about Him. You cannot then call yourself an atheist or unbeliever. For you cannot think or say: Life has no depth! Life itself is shallow. Being itself is surface only.
>
> . . . The name of this infinite and inexhaustible ground of history is *God*. That is what the word means, and it is that to which the words *Kingdom of God* and *Divine Providence* point. And if these words do not have much meaning for you, translate them and speak of the depth of history, of the ground and aim of our social life, and of what you take seriously without reservation in your moral and political activities. Perhaps you should call this depth *hope*, simply hope (Paul Tillich, *The Shaking of the Foundations*, NY: Charles Scribner's Sons, 1953, pp. 57, 59).

As is true with most themes in existentialism, Tillich's idea of God is deeply colored by the existential theme of subjectivity. Subjectivity is so important in existentialism that it almost becomes the most important theme, affecting all other existential thought.

Grace

Tillich not only redefined the traditional view of God, but he also put an existential interpretation to the concept of grace. His grace is universal, subjective, and flows from and to each individual. When he talks of the "acceptance" of grace, he is not talking about the forgiveness of God made possible by the sacrifice of Jesus Christ upon the cross. He is talking about the subjective experience of acceptance that one feels during a crisis.

> Grace strikes us when we are in great pain and restlessness . . . It strikes us when we feel that our separation is deeper than usual, because we have violated another life, a life which we loved, or from which we were estranged. It strikes us when our disgust for our own being, our indifference, our weakness, our hostility, and our lack of direction and composure have become intolerable to us . . . . Sometimes at that moment a wave of light breaks into our darkness, and it is as though a voice were saying: "You are accepted. *You are accepted*, accepted by that which is greater than you, and the name of which you do not know. Do not ask for the name now; perhaps you will find it later . . . . *Simply accept the fact that you are accepted!*" In the

> light of this grace we perceive the power of grace in our relation to others and to ourselves. . . . We experience the grace of being able to accept the life of another, even if it be hostile and harmful to us, for, through grace, we know that it belongs to the same Ground to which we belong, and by which we have been accepted (ibid., pp. 161, 162).

In summary, we can see that Tillich's concerns (just a few of which have been highlighted here) are common to existential themes and that his applications of those themes to religion change the very essence or fundamentals of Christian belief. It cannot be denied that he was a religious existentialist. But it is also true that he was not an evangelical Christian, committed to the biblical fundamentals of our faith.

Gabriel Marcel (1889-1973)

Another religious philosopher who had strong influence in the growth of French existentialism was Gabriel Marcel (1889-1973). Marcel, a French Catholic existentialist, criticized many of his fellow existentialists. His primary philosophical loyalty to existentialism seemed to be the stress he placed on the value of the individual. Philosopher Anthony Flew comments:

> . . . Marcel considered existentialism to be compatible with Christian doctrines. The aim of life is "communication" between men as well as between man and God, but relationships must be based on and retain the freedom and uniqueness of individuals, not be dependent on the joint acceptance of rules and goals (Anthony Flew, ed., *A Dictionary of Philosophy*, NY: St. Martin's Press, 1982, p. 204).

Jean T. Wilde and William Kimmel make the following additional appraisal of Marcel:

> Gabriel Marcel, a Christian existentialist, shares with the atheist existentialist Sartre the responsibility for the further development in France of that trend in philosophy represented by this anthology. A convert to Roman Catholicism, Marcel has nevertheless maintained a philosophical independence from the official philosophy of the church and has developed original avenues of thought that bear the unmistakable stamp of their author's temperament and spirit. He is not only a philosopher but also a successful dramatist and a fine musician (Jean T. Wilde and William Kimmel, eds., trans., *The Search for Being*, NY: The Noonday Press, 1962, p. 417).

It is important to remember that while Wilde and Kimmel, as well as Flew, note Marcel's alignment with Christianity, they also note that this alignment was not with historic Christianity. Marcel actually denied those doctrines evangelicals consider vital.

Marcel's philosophy was much less systematic than other existentialists such as Tillich, so we will just touch on some of his concerns. Marcel was more of an observer than a shaper of philosophy or theology. His greatest concerns were those which were involved in existentialism and which earned him a place among existentialist thinkers.

> Rather than systematic discourses, Marcel's works are collections of observations and notes. Avoiding the traditional metaphysical categories and principles, his thought revolves around a number of root ideas which are not so much ideas as modes of concrete experience: estrangement, nostalgia, and homecoming; presence and absence; appeal and response; fidelity and betrayal; availability and unavailability; despair, recollection, courage, and hope. It is within the framework of these modes of experience that human life unfolds and it is here, rather than in the abstract manipulations of technical reason, that Being as personality and community can reveal itself. In reflection upon these dimensions of experience, Marcel evokes a sense of the mystery that envelops and unfolds within experience, that informs, illumines and fulfills experience, the mystery that is not alien to existence because it is itself that from which existence has its being. By recovering this inner bond between existence and mystery, one uncovers the source of his own meaning and creative power (ibid., p. 419).

I. M. Bochenski gives an excellent discussion of the basic ideas of Marcel. He has done such a good job of summarizing Marcel that we will quote from him extensively:

> Marcel holds that being-an-object and existence are two entirely different dimensions of being. This is seen most clearly in the fundamental problem of embodiment (*incarnation*). The relation between my body and myself cannot be described as either being or having. I *am* my body, yet I cannot identify myself with it. The question about embodiment has led Marcel to a rigorous distinction between the *problem* and the *mystery*. A problem concerns what lies wholly before me, something which I scan objectively as an observer. A mystery, on the other hand, is "something in which I am involved (*engagé*)." Only mysteries are of any philosophic relevance and thus philosophy must be transobjective, personal, dramatic, indeed tragic. "I am not

witnessing a spectacle": we should remind ourselves of this every day, says Marcel. The possibility of suicide is the point of departure of every genuine metaphysics. Such a metaphysics must be neither rational or intuitive. It is the result of a kind of second reflection (*réflexion seconde*).

Marcel has not worked out this metaphysics, but he has adumbrated its methodology. It is to give an answer to the basic ontological demand, namely, that there must be being, there must be something which cannot be explained away in some easy way as, for example, psychoanalysis explains away psychic phenomena. We are certain that there is being through the mysterious reality of the "I am"—not through *cogito ergo sum*. In this way the opposition of subject and object, of idealism, is overcome. Human reality reveals itself as the reality of a *homo viator*, of being which is always in process of becoming. Every philosophy which misinterprets this truth, which tries to explain man by means of a system, is incapable of understanding man.

We are led to the understanding of human being above all through the study of human relationships which are signified by judgments in the second person, in the *thou*. These unobjective thou-relationships are creative, for through them I create myself and also help another to create his own freedom. Here Marcel is close to the Jewish philosopher Martin Buber (b. 1878) who had enunciated similar theses even before Marcel. The center of the thou-relationship is faithfulness (*fidélité*). It appears as the embodiment of a higher free actuality, since the faithful one creates himself in freedom. Hope is even more basic than faithfulness, for the latter is built upon hope. Marcel holds that hope has ontological significance. It shows that the victory of death in the world is merely apparent and not final. Marcel regards his doctrine of hope as the most important result of his work. Here he departs radically from Sartre and Heidegger and apparently even from Jaspers.

The human thou can also be objectivized and become an it. But for this there is a definite limit, behind which stands the absolute thou which can no longer be taken as an object, namely God. We cannot through reason prove the existence of God. One encounters God on the same plane as the other, the plane of the thou, in loving and in honoring through participation in true being which may already take its rise in the questioning attitude of the philosopher (Bochenski, *Eurpoean Philosophy*, p. 183, 184).

The Secular Existentialists

By far the largest group of thinkers categorized as extentialists are those with no religious orientation at all, the secular existentialists. Some of them ignore religion completely, others are forcefully atheistic. The secular existentialists are concerned with the same themes as the religious existentialists, but their presuppostions and belief systems preclude any supernatural or any idea of God.

In our overview, we will examine three secular existentialists: Martin Heidegger, Karl Jaspers and Jean-Paul Sartre.

Martin Heidegger (1889-1976)

Martin Heidegger was one of the most influential promoters of contemporary existentialism. He wrote in German but his works have been translated into English. His most famous, *Being and Time*, has become one of the most popular expressions of English/American existentialism in the philosophical world. Alston and Nakhnikian note the scope of Heidegger's spreading influence:

> In Latin America and Europe, excluding, of course, the Soviet Union and her European satellites, one of the dominant contemporary philosophers is Heidegger. Heidegger's influence ranges widely over philosophers, theologians (including Paul Tillich), and certain psychotherapists. In the English-speaking world, too, there are philosophers who regard Heidegger with as much respect as do his Continental and Latin-American admirers (Alston and Nakhnikian, *Readings*, p. 679).

Heidegger's writings had a great effect on both the religious existentialist Rudolph Bultmann, who attempted to build a theology from Heideggerian existentialism, and Jean-Paul Sartre, the French secular existentialist and novelist.

Heidegger studied under the philosopher Edmund Husserl before he became rector of Freiburg University in 1933. His main treatise, *Sein und Zeit*(*Being and Time*), was published in 1927. Although *Being and Time* reflected the influence Husserl and Kierkegaard made on Heidegger, it also showed he differed from those men in some important ways.

Heidegger's existentialism is unique and complex. It is difficult for even professional philosophers to understand:

> Heidegger is an extremely original thinker. The problem of his historical affiliations is not of primary concern here and we need only mention that he borrows his method from Husserl, that he is in many ways influenced by Dilckey, and that his general

> thesis is largely inspired by Kierkegaard. Heidegger is equipped with an unusual knowledge of the great philosophers of the past, among whom he frequently quotes Aristotle, although he interprets him in very arbitrary fashion. A stir was caused by the volume which he devoted to Kant, *Kant und das Problem der Metaphysik* (1929).
>
> Few philosophers are so hard to understand as Heidegger (Bochenski, *European Philosophy*, p. 161).

Because Heidegger's philosophy is so difficult to understand, interpretations of his thought vary and even contradict one another. Philosopher/historian A. Robert Caponigri remarks:

> Heidegger's thought has given rise to extensive interpretations, varying much among themselves and frequently at variance with the line of exegesis which Heidegger himself has suggested. From the point of view of doctrine and interests, his thought falls into two phases. The line of demarcation is drawn (but not too sharply), . . . by the Holderlin lecture in 1936. The first phase centers about the great work of 1927: *Sein und Zeit*. This work is still considered as presenting the essential Heidegger. It most clearly exhibits his originality as a thinker in his "existential analysis" of human behavior with respect to the "unveiling of truth" and his "ontological" mode of treating phenomenology. It is the basis for the wide influence he has enjoyed. The second phase possesses no strict unity but shows Heidegger's concern with a number of themes, both historical and analytical, stemming from his main concern: being and truth (A. Robert Caponigri, *A History of Western Philosophy: Philosophy from the Age of Positivism to the Age of Analysis*, Notre Dame, in: University of Notre Dame Press, 1971, p. 264).

Along with the difficulty in understanding Heidegger, and the added difficulty of interpretation, we find that Heidegger did not view himself as an existentialist!

> Heidegger believes that the term "existentialist" does not apply to his philosophy. . . Heidegger grants that "existentialism" is an apt label for what Sartre represents, but not for his own position. Heidegger is interested in Being. He approaches the problem of Being through the study of *Dasein*, Heidegger's word for human existence, "the being of what we ourselves are" (Alston and Nakhnikian, *Readings*, p. 680).

Because of these problems, we will not deal extensively with Heidegger although he bears mentioning because of his influence on other existentialists. Recognizing our limits of space and purpose, we will confine our discussion to three concerns of Heidegger: *Dasein, angst,* and *death*. The reader is referred to the bibliography for books that deal more extensively with Heidegger.

Dasein

The most important concept unique to Heidegger's system is *Dasein* (a word Heidegger used to refer to the human being, or the existing-ness of the human, which causes or becomes his essence). William Sahakian describes *Dasein*:

> *Dasein*. The idea of Being is an old one to a philosopher grounded in Scholasticism, as Heidegger was. But Heidegger was interested in the meaning of Being, its sense, or its purpose—i.e., what renders it intelligible. Furthermore, he was interested primarily in the *human* Being, for the nature of the human Being leads to other levels of Being or reality. Only *Dasein* (his term for the human Being) can be said to have or not to have meaning; hence *Being* is meaningful solely in terms of human existence.
>
> *Dasein* (being-there), that is, the human Being or the human existent, Heidegger identified as: (1) concern (*Sorge*), (2) being-toward-death (*Sein zum Tode*), (3) existence (*Existenz*), and (4) moods (*Stimmungen*). The human Being's essence is in his existence, for numerous possibilities are open to him whereby he may choose differnent kinds of Being for himself. The possibilities of what he may become are the pivotal points by which the human Being is oriented. Heidegger was greatly interested in interpreting time in terms of temporality; consequently, in addition to the problem of Being (*Dasein*), time is of utmost importance. Accordingly, his interest was in the Being and temporality of *Dasein* (human existence) (Sahakian, *Philosophy*, p. 349).

Angst

Angst is another term with heavy existential meaning for Heidegger. The German word refers to anxiety, dread and hopeless fear of the future. This concept is important to Heidegger because it forms the impetus for much of human metaphysical development. It is the goad toward human existential encounter.

> In existentialist philosophy, (angst is) the dread occasioned by man's realization that his existence is open towards an undetermined future, the emptiness of which must be filled by his free-

ly chosen actions. Anxiety characterizes the human state, which entails constant confrontation with possibility and the need for decision, with the concomitant burden of responsibility (Flew, *Philsophy*, p. 13).

Death

As it is with most existential thought, death is important in Heidegger's system. His secular (non-supernatural) presuppositions, and his commitment to existence preceding essence give Heidegger no view of reality for an individual before birth or after death. According to his scheme, the man who recognizes this fact, freely accepts its inevitability, and seeks nothing beyond, is then free to choose his own existence. He is no longer bound by fear of death or imaginary retributive punishment after death. He is able to choose his actions, thereby choosing his existence and ultimately his essence. This is man with dignity.

> For Heidegger, man is the being that knows he is going to die. He dies not only at the end of life, but every day of it. Death is certain, yet indefinite. Because it is inevitable it marks the contingency of life. Life is cast up between nothing and nothing. Death is its boundary and is its supreme possibility. To freely accept death, to live in its presence, and to acknowledge that for it there is no substitute and into it one must go alone, is to escape from all illusions and to achieve genuine dignity and authentic existence (Fuller, *Philosophy*, p. 608).

Jean-Paul Sartre (1905-1980)

The man who most popularized an atheistic brand of existentialism was the French philosopher, Jean-Paul Sartre. Sartre's major work, *Being and Nothingness*, was written in 1943 while he was a prisoner of the Germans during World War II. Some of his other writings, including *Existentialism is Humanism* and the novel, *No Exit*, reflect an indebtedness to both Kierkegaard and Heidegger. Sartre's great ability enabled him to have a clear understanding of the history of philosophy. Marjorie Greene reports:

> [Sartre] does indeed use the thinkers of the past (and present) for his own ends, but at the same time he sees them with extraordinary clarity. In his references, say, to Kant or Spinoza, he not only uses their thought as a springboard for his own, but also exhibits a solid and scholarly penetration into their

principles and views. His relation to Marx is less straightforward, as we shall see, but in general one finds in his philosophical works an interweaving of themes in which the original strands stand out for themselves with unusual distinctness, while at the same time they are being worked into a characteristically Sartrean pattern (Marjorie Green, *Sartre*, NY: Franklin Watts, Inc., 1973, p. 33).

Absurdity

One major tenet of Sartre's existentialism is that life is absurd. In his novel, *Nausea*, Sartre brings out the absurdity of life through his main character, Roquentin. Robert Davidson writes,

> The story of Roquentin, the hero of *Nausea*, is not told as an end in itself. Actually it expresses Sartre's own view concerning human existence. This story provides a descriptive or phenomenological account of a man's growing realization of the absurdity of human life in itself, and of his awakening to the fact that if a man's life is to have any meaning or purpose, the individual himself must confer that meaning upon it. A sense of the absurd, the absurdity of life and of man himself, permeates Sartre's early existentialism. In *Nausea* he portrays this as an immediate insight in one's own experience. As he sat in a public park one day, staring at the long black roots of an old chestnut tree, Roquentin became acutely aware of the absurdity of his own existence:
>
> "Absurdity was not an idea in my head nor the sound of a voice. It was this long, lean, wooden snake curled up at my feet—snake or claw or talon or root, it was all the same. Without formulating anything I knew that I had found the clue to my existence, to my nausea to my life. And indeed everything I have ever grasped since that moment comes back to this fundamental absurdity" (Robert F. Davidson, *Philosophies Men Live By*, NY: Holt, Rinehart and Winston, Inc., 1974, p. 362).

Man is Autonomous

The absurdity of the universe leads Sartre to another major tenet of existentialism; namely, that man is autonomous. Sartre wrote:

> The existentialist, on the contrary, thinks it very distressing that God does not exist, because all possibility of finding values in a heaven of ideas disappears along with Him; there can no longer be an *a priori* Good, since there is no infinite and perfect consciousness to think it. Nowhere is it written that the Good

> exists, that we must be honest, that we must not lie: because the fact is we are on a plane where there are only men. Dostoevsky said, 'If God didn't exist, everything would be possible.' That is the very starting point of existentialism. Indeed, everything is permissible if God does not exist, and as a result man is forlorn, because neither within him nor without does he find anything to cling to. He can't start making excuses for himself. In other words, there is no determinism, man is free, man is freedom. On the other hand, if God does not exist, we find no values or commands to turn to which legitimize our conduct. So, in the bright realm of values, we have no excuse behind us, nor justification before us. We are alone, with no excuses (Jean-Paul Sartre, *Existentialism and Human Emotions*, NY: The Citadel Press, n.d., pp. 22, 23).

Freedom

Man comes into the scene and defines himself. He lives in absolute freedom. Sartre states:

> That is the idea I shall try to convey when I say that man is condemned to be free. Condemned, because he did not create himself, yet, in other respects is free; because, once thrown into the world, he is responsible for everything he does. The existentialist does not believe in the power of passion. He will never agree that a sweeping passion is a ravaging torrent which fatally leads a man to certain acts and is therefore an excuse. He thinks that man is responsible for his passion (ibid., p. 23).

Existence Before Essence

Another major tenet of Sartre's existentialism is that existence precedes essence. This means that man, by his own choices, defines his character, his essence and the person he is becoming. His choices determine his make-up. Sartre argues:

> Atheistic existentialism, which I represent, is more coherent. It states that if God does not exist, there is at least one being in whom existence precedes essence, a being who exists before he can be defined by any concept, and that this being is man, or as Heidegger says, human reality. What is meant here by saying that existence precedes essence? It means that, first of all, man exists, turns up, appears on the scene, and, only afterwards, defines himself. If man, as the existentialist conceives him, in indefinable, it is because at first he is nothing. Only afterward will he be something, and he himself will have made what he will be. Thus, there is no human nature, since there is no God to conceive it. Not only is man what he conceives

> himself to be, but he is also only what he wills himself to be after this thrust toward existence (ibid., pp. 15-16).

In *Being and Nothingness*, Sartre states

> Human freedom precedes essence in man and makes it possible. The essence of the human being is suspended in freedom (Jean-Paul Sartre, *Being and Nothingness*, NY: Philosophical Library, Inc., 1956, p. 25).

He continues with the ramififcations of this assertion:

> [It is that] choice that is called "will." But if existence really does precede essence, man is responsible for what he is. Thus, existentialism's first move is to make every man aware of what he is and to make the full responsibility of his existence rest on him. And when we say that a man is responsible for himself, we do not only mean that he is responsible for his own individuality, but that he is responsible for all men (ibid., p. 16).

Fulfillment

Sartre believed that man could receive his own self-fulfillment, as Sahakian reports:

> Notwithstanding the pessimistic views in most of Sartre's writings his existentialism ends on a note of optimism, for his *Existentialism is Humanism* concludes with the declaration that existentialism does not plunge man into despair but is an optimistic doctrine of action, that man is his own lawmaker, a creator of values, living in a human universe of human subjectivity, and capable of self-fulfillment (Sahakian, *Philosophy*, p. 357).

Thus, man makes his own fulfillment. Those who try to accomplish this through religion are guilty of bad faith, as Flew defines:

> *Bad faith.* In the existentialism of Sartre, a form of deception of self and others; the attempt to rationalize human existence through religion, science, or any belief in operative forces that impose meaning and coherence. Man shapes his own destiny through a succession of free choices for which he is totally responsible. In 'bad faith' he denies the necessity of relying on his own moral insight and fallible will, trying to escape the burden of responsibility by regarding himself as the passive subject of outside influences, and his actions as being predetermined by these rather than freely chosen by himself (Flew, *Philosophy*, p. 35).

Forlornness

One of the major themes Sartre dealt with is also (not surprisingly) one for which he is perhaps best known, the theme of forlornness. It arises out of existential individuality and subjectivity. In some ways, it resembles Kierkegaard's second and unsatisfying stage, where man realizes he is alone, determines an ethic, but has nothing on which to depend. Sartre himself presented a moving description of this forlornness in the previously cited *Existentialism and Human Emotion*:

> To give you an example which will enable you to understand forlornness better, I shall cite the case of one of my students who came to see me under the following circumstnaces: his father was on bad terms with his mother, and moreover, was inclined to be a collaborationist; his older brother had been killed in the German offensive of 1940, and the young man, with somewhat immature but generous feelings, wanted to avenge him. His mother lived alone with him, very much upset by the half-treason of her husband and the death of her older son; the boy was her only consolation.
>
> The boy was faced with the choice of leaving for England and joining the Free French Forces—that is, leaving his mother behind—or remaining with his mother and helping her to carry on. He was fully aware that the woman lived only for him and that his going-off—and perhaps his death—would plunge her into despair. He was also aware that every act that he did for his mother's sake was a sure thing, in the sense that it was helping her to carry on, whereas every effort he made toward going off and fighting was an uncertain move which might run aground and prove completely useless; for example, on his way to England he might, while passing through Spain, be detained indefinitely in a Spanish camp; he might reach England or Algiers and be stuck in an office at a desk job. As a result, he was faced with two very different kinds of action: one, concrete, immediate, but concerning only one individual; the other concerned an incomparably vaster group, a national collectivity, but for that very reason was dubious, and might be interrupted en route. And, at the same time, he was wavering between two kinds of ethics. On the one hand, an ethics of sympathy, of personal devotion; on the other, a broader ethics, but one whose efficacy was more dubious. He had to choose between the two.
>
> Who could help him choose? Christian doctrine? No. Christian doctrine says, "Be charitable, love your neighbor, take the more rugged path, etc., etc." But which is the more rugged path? Whom should he love as a brother? The fighting man or his

> mother? Which does the greater good, the vague act of fighting in a group, or the concrete one of helping a particular human being to go on living? Who can decide *a priori*? Nobody. No book of ethics can tell him. The Kantian ethics says, "Never treat any person as a means, but as an end." Very well, if I stay with my mother, I'll treat her as an end and not as a means; but by virtue of this very fact, I'm running the risk of treating the people around me who are fighting, as means; and, conversely, if I go to join those who are fighting, I'll be treating them as an end, and, by doing that, I run the risk of treating my mother as a means.
>
> If values are vague, and if they are always too broad for the concrete and specific case that we are considering, the only thing left for us is to trust our instincts. That's what this young man tried to do; and when I saw him, he said, "In the end, feeling is what counts. I ought to choose whichever pushes me in one direction. If I feel that I love my mother enough to sacrifice everything else for her—my desire for vengeance, for action, for adventure—then I'll stay with her. If, on the contrary, I feel that my love for my mother isn't enough, I'll leave.
>
> But how is the value of a feeling determined? What gives his feeling for his mother value? Precisely the fact that he remained with her. I may say that I like so-and-so well enough to sacrifice a certain amount of money for him, but I may say so only if I've done it. I may say "I love my mother well enough to remain with her" if I have remained with her. The only way to determine the value of this affection is, precisely, to perform an act which confirms and defines it. But, since I require this affection to justify my act, I find myself caught in a vicious circle. (Sartre, *Existentialism*, pp. 24-27).

From this we can see the futility inherent in Sartre's existential thought. Since "existence precedes essence," and the individual is enveloped within "subjectivity" and must find his essence of "authenticity," he is truly alone. Many people have embraced existentialism for a time, sincerely thinking that its view of life is accurate. However, many leave existentialism because it offers a solution, meaning, and commitment which is not truly satisfying. Even Sartre, toward the end of his life, swung very close to theistic commitment. The magazine *National Review* reported it this way:

> Throughout his mature career, the philosopher Jean-Paul Sartre was a militant atheist. Politically, although he quarreled with Marxist materialism, his rhetoric was often indistinguishable from the most heavy-handed Stalinist boilerplate.

However, during the philosopher's last months there were some surprising developments. In 1980, nearing his death, by then blind, decrepit, but still in full possession of his faculties, Sartre came very close to belief in God, perhaps even more than very close.

The story can be told briefly, and perhaps reverently. An ex-Maoist, Pierre Victor, shared much of Sartre's time toward the end. In the early spring of 1980 the two had a dialogue in the pages of the *ultra-gauchiste Nouvel Observateur*. It is sufficient to quote a single sentence from what Sartre said then to measure the degree of his acceptance of the grace of God and the creatureliness of man: "I do not feel that I am the product of chance, a speck of dust in the universe, but someone who was expected, prepared, prefigured. In short, a being whom only a Creator could put here: and this idea of a creating hand refers to God."

Students of existentialism, the atheistic branch, will note that in this one sentence Sartre disavowed his entire system, his *engagements*, his whole life. Voltaire converted on his deathbed; one never knows, the brilliant old rascal is supposed to have said. Sartre did not convert, at least outwardly, but came to understand. Everything ought to be forgiven him.

The epilogue is much less edifying. His mistress, Simone de Beauvoir, behaved like a bereaved widow during the funeral. Then she published *La cérémonie des adieux* in which she turned vicious, attacking Sartre. He resisted Victor's seduction, she recounts, then he yielded. "How should one explain this senile act of a turncoat?" she asks stupidly. And she adds: "All my friends, all the Sartrians, and the editorial team of *Les Temps Modernes* supported me in my consternation."

Mme. de Beauvoir's consternation *v.* Sartre's conversion. The balance is infinitely heavier on the side of the blind, yet seeing, old man. (*National Review*, June 11, 1982, p. 677).

Karl Jaspers (1883-1969)

Karl Jaspers began his academic career by studying law at Heidelberg and Munich. He later studied medicine at several German universities and soon made important contributions to pathological and psychiatric research. He was professor of philosophy at Heidelberg from 1921 until the Nazis came into power. After World War II he returned to Heidelberg and in 1948 he moved to Basel. He was one of the foremost representatives of extentialism.

B. A. G. Fuller comments upon those who influenced Jaspers' thought:

> His philosophical activity was influenced from the beginning by careful studies of Kant and Hegel, but Kierkegaard and Nietzsche have dominated his thought by directing it constantly upon the problem of the human condition. His philosophy has been more than anything else an attempt to answer their question of the nature of human existence. His answers reflect his Kantianism. (Fuller, *Philosophy*, p. 604).

One aspect of Jaspers' philosophy is that it is more balanced than that of some of his existentialist comrades. I. M. Bochenski reports

> The thought of Karl Jaspers is on the whole much more balanced than that of the majority of his fellow existentialists; for example, he critically analyzes their view of science, to which he accords a far more important place than they do. His books contain a wealth of remarkable analyses and are written in comparatively simple language free from the characteristic neologisms which make the other authors so difficult to read. An obvious concern for metaphysics and a sort of natural theology also serve to distinguish him from the others who share the same label. Even so, he exhibits the fundamental attitudes and convictions common to all existentialists (Bochenski, *European Philosophy*, p. 185).

His Method

In 1932 Jaspers completed a major philosophical work entitled, *Philosophie*. In it he examined in depth the common philosophical method, relating it to his own brand of existentialism. Robert A. Caponigri comments:

> Jaspers' philosophical thought proper begins to emerge with the work *Philosophie* and is developed in the subsequent works. These works do not, however, constitute a progressive movement toward a systematic position. Jaspers' thought is thematic, not systematic. The basic themes of his thought are three: 1) science and its relation to man's understanding of himself, 2) existence, and 3) transcendence. The most fruitful approach to Jaspers' thought lies in the exploration of his meditative enrichment of these themes. (Caponigri, *Philosophy*, p. 257).

His Philosophy

Jean T. Wilde and William Kimmel sum up the philosophy of Karl Jaspers:

> For Jaspers philosophy is not the attempt to give definitive form to a body of knowledge about man in his universe. Philosophy

is rather a way, an activity of the human mind moving toward the ultimate truth which can never become an object of knowledge, but which can be encountered in that process of thought which he calls "transcending thinking." Truth is always on the way, always in movement and never becomes final, not even in its most wonderful crystallizations. Thought is never at rest in its own content.

God, Man, and the World, while they may become objects of our attention can never become objects of knowledge. Their authentic being, their fundamental reality, always recedes beyond the limits of objectification, defying confinement and circumscription. They are, therefore, objects of encounter during the process of reflective thinking but encountered at the limits or boundaries of knowledge. The objects of knowledge or reflection, whether the products of scientific, aesthetic, mythical, philosophical, psychological, or merely common-sense experience are not ends and results but limiting forms whose reality lies not in their positive form or content but in their power to point beyond themselves toward Transcendence—the goal of philosophical thought.

But just as God—Transcendence, the all encompassing One in which and from which all things have their being and meaning—transcends objectification, so also the Self in its authenticity, its *Existenz*, can never become an object for itself. One encounters the Self at the "boundary situations" of existence, at the limits of knowledge and action, at those points where all knowledge and action fails, or founders—in the presence of absolute chance, conflict, suffering, guilt, death. At these boundary situations of finite existence one is driven either to despair or to a discovery of authentic Selfhood in freedom. In other words, in the concrete situation, where the forms of knowledge fail, the formulas do not apply, the path is no longer predetermined, one is forced to decide, and in this free decision out of the Self one discovers the true Self, the Being which one is.

Between the Being that I am (*Existenz*) and the Being that is the all (*Transcendence*) lies the World embodied in the constructed and interpreted forms of knowledge. This World, however, is also evanescent and, in a sense, unstable, but its forms serve as a mediation between the Self that I am and the Transcendence toward which my thought moves. As *forms* of mediation the forms of knowledge of the World are indispensable; but as forms of *mediation* none is final or absolute or binding. Their status is that of "cyphers," symbols that are open to Transcendence and through which reflection can encounter Transcendence. Only when they are "interpreted" as a cypher-script of Being rather than accepted as self-sufficient objects of knowledge is their status and that of the World they embody understood. But the interpretation itself is never final or accomplished. Nor can there be an interpretation for man-in-general. Each individual in his encounter with the World must interpret them anew, for only in the act of interpretation does the Transcendence which hovers around the forms reveal itself through them. There is necessary, then, both the expectant receptivity of the Self to the cypher and the recognition of the forms of knowledge as being cyphers of Being.

True philosophy, then, for Jaspers, is a hovering (*Schweben*) of the mind around the given forms of knowledge and the forming forms of one's own thought, a gliding of thought in expectant search for that truth about the Self, the World and God which reveals itself as the Being that is for the Being that I am (Wilde and Kimmel, *Search*, p. 451-3).

Jaspers and Sartre

F. H. Heinemann has compared the existential philosophies of Jaspers and Sartre, and he shows some interesting differences between them:

Jaspers	Sartre
Keep space open for the Comprehensive!	There is no Comprehensive.
Do not identify yourself with an object of your knowledge!	Commit yourself!
Do not reject any form of the Comprehensive!	Reject all those forms which restrict your liberty!
Do not accept any defamation of existence!	Describe reality in its ugliness, absurdity and obscenity!
Do not allow yourself to be cut off from the Transcendent!	You are cut off from the Transcendent, for it is non-existent.

(Heinemann, *Existentialism*, p. 129).

Despite the differences between Jaspers and Sartre (and, in fact, among many existentialists), there are common themes that run throughout their philosophies.

Christian Response

The themes of existentialism are themes that the God of the Bible addresses in His Word. God is concerned about individuals. God is concerned about an individual's happiness, contentment and inner peace. God is concerned about an individual's fulfillment. However, existentialism is not biblical Christianity. Though not a Christian, philosopher Hazel Barnes notes that distinction:

> My first objection to the theological claims of Tillich, Robinson, Bonhoeffer, and Bultmann—to use them as examples and speaking of what they share in common without implying that they are in full agreement—is that they claim to be Christian while denying what has been essential in Christianity whereas they subtly retain Christian assumptions when they profess to establish philosophical truths independent of sectarian commitments.
>
> In their plea for a revolution in Christian thought, these theologians seem at times to argue for a position scarcely discernible from naturalism. The idea of a God "out there" somewhere in or beyond space, or the concept of any Being which is separate from us and the world is as offensive to Bishop Robinson as the medieval God who dwelt "up there" in Dante's three-level universe. Tillich argues against all use of "supernatural" concepts of God. Bultmann urges that we must "demythologize." Bonhoeffer suggests that Christianity should advance to the point where it no longer needs the "religious premise," that the Christian must "plunge himself into the life of a godless world, without attempting to gloss over its ungodliness with a veneer of religion or trying to transfigure it" (Barnes, *Ethics*, pp. 382, 383).

Bochenski gives another slant to a critical look at existentialism. He talks about some of the philosophical problems posed but not answered by the usual existential concepts:

> As often happens, existentialism has gone too far in the rejection, inherently justified, of the past. For many existentialist philosophers there seems to be nothing in principle worth considering except those . . . questions of fate we have already alluded to. Their whole philosophy seems to center on death, suffering, failure. Thereby they neglect another essential factor in European culture, namely that sense of the objective and scientific which the Greeks had in such eminent degree. Often existentialism goes so far . . . that it seems to be more an Indian than a European philosophy, that is, a kind of thought which seems to be exclusively, even in its logic, a kind of therapeutic device. It is for such reasons that existentialism encounters justified reproach among many, perhaps most, serious European philosophers.
>
> Another unique trait of existentialist philosophy . . . is its definite technical philosophical character. Here many valuable insights and results are discernible. Unquestionably philosophy

> has been enriched by numerous superior analyses in psychology and phenomenology, and some fields have in fact been subjected to study for the first time through these efforts, for example, pure personal relationships between human beings—"being-with-another," "being-for-another," "thou," "communication." A study of problems has thus arisen which constitutes a definite advancement in philosophy. Equally fundamental are the critical attacks on positivism and on idealism by the existentialists. Against the first they have successfully defended the irreducibility of human existence to matter, and respecting the second they have asserted with great power and conviction the priority of existence to thought. They have occupied themselves with ontology in various ways and some have not only worked it out in detail but have capped their efforts with a metaphysics (Bochenski, *European Philosophy*, p. 199).

Christianity is based on a completely different set of presuppositions from those of existentialism. While existentialism stresses subjective inner experience, Christianity links subjective inner experience with objective and testable supernatural events in history (such as the resurrection of Jesus Christ) and with God-given and God-developed reason. Biblical Christians have faith. Existentialists also have faith. But faith, however sincere, is not enough. Faith must have an object and that object must be worthy of faith. Jesus Christ alone, the creator and sustainer of the universe and every individual in it, is worthy of ultimate faith.

We have dealt with the historicity of the Christian faith and its reasonableness in previous works (see, for example, Josh's *Evidence, More than a Carpenter,* and *The Resurrection Factor*; and Josh and Don's *Reasons* and *Answers*). Christianity presents a cohesive world view which fits the reality around us. Existentialism does not. We are convinced that Christianity alone makes the greatest sense out of the world we live in and out of our own inner thoughts and feelings. Christian philosopher Richard Purtill has capably summarized our perspective:

> . . . reason is on the side of Christianity. . . . If we begin to ask fundamental questions about the universe, and follow the argument where it leads us, then it will lead us to belief in God; that if we examine the evidence of history and of human experience, we will be compelled to acknowledge that the only satisfactory explanation of the evidence leads us to Christianity.

Such Christians admit that there is still a gap between intellectual assent and commitment to a Christian way of life, but they believe that reason is neither opposed to such a commitment or irrelevant to it—rather, it is the best possible ground for it (Richard Purtill, *C. S. Lewis's Case for the Christian Faith*, San Francisco: Harper and Row, Publishers, 1981, pp. 12, 13).

Existentialism Bibliography

Alston, William P. and George Nakhnikian, *Readings in Twentieth Century Philosophy*. NY: The Free Press, 1963.

Angeles, Peter A., *Dictionary of Philosophy*. NY: Harper and Row, Publishers, 1981.

Avey, Albert E., *Handbook in the History of Philosophy*. NY: Barnes and Noble, Inc., 1961.

Barnes, Hazel E., *An Existentialist Ethics*. Chicago: University of Chicago Press, 1978.

Bochenski, I. M., *Contemporary European Philosophy*. Berkeley and Los Angeles: University of California Press, 1954.

Brown, James, *Kierkegaard, Heidegger, Buber and Barth*. NY: Collier Books, 1955.

Caponigri, A. Robert, *A History of Western Philosophy: Philosophy from the Age of Positivism to the Age of Analysis*. Notre Dame, IN: University of Notre Dame Press, 1971.

Collins, James, *The Existentialist*. Chicago: Henry Regnery Co., 1952.

Davidson, Robert F., *Philosophies Men Live By*. NY: Holt, Rinehart and Winston, Inc., 1974.

Edwards, Rem B., *Reason and Religion*. NY: Harcourt Brace Jovanovich, Inc., 1972.

Flew, Antony, *A Dictionary of Philosophy*. NY: St. Martin's Press, 1982.

Frankl, Viktor E., *Man's Search for Meaning*. NY: Pocket Books, 1963.

Frost, S. E., Jr., *Basic Teachings of the Great Philosophers*. Garden City, NY: Doubleday and Company, Inc., 1962.

Fuller, B. A. G., *A History of Philosophy*. NY: Holt, Rinehart and Winston, 1955.

Geisler, Norman L. and Paul D. Feinberg, *Introduction to Philosophy*. Grand Rapids, MI: Baker Book House, 1980.

Greene, Marjorie, *Sartre*. NY: Franklin Watts, Inc., 1973.

Heidegger, Martin, *On Time and Being*. NY: Harper and Row, Publishers, 1972.

Heinemann, F. H., *Existentialism and the Modern Predicament*. NY: Harper and Row, Publishers, 1953.

Herberg, Will, *Four Existentialist Theologians*. Garden City, NY: Doubleday and Company, Inc., 1958.

Horvath, Nicholas A., *Philosophy*. Woodbury, NY: Barron's Educational Series, 1974.

Hunnex, Milton D., *Existentialism and Christian Belief*. Chicago, IL: Moody Press, 1969.

James, William, *The Varieties of Religious Experience*. NY: The New American Library, Inc., 1958.

Kaufmann, Walter, *Existentialism from Dostoevsky to Sartre*. NY: The World Publishing Co., 1956.

______________, *Existentialism, Religion and Death*. NY: The New American Library, Inc., 1976.

Kierkegaard, Soren, *Attack upon Christendom*. Princeton, NJ: Princeton University Press, 1944, 1968.

______________, *The Point of View for My Work as An Author*. NY: Harper and Row, Publishers, 1962.

Marias, Julian, *History of Philosophy*. NY: Dover Publications, Inc., 1967.

Purtill, Richard L., *C. S. Lewis's Case for the Christian Faith*. San Francisco: Harper and Row, Publishers, 1981.

______________, *Thinking About Ethics*. Englewood Cliffs, NJ: Prentice-Hall, Inc., 1976.

Runes, Dagobert D., ed., *Dictionary of Philosophy*. Totowa, NJ: Littlefield, Adams and Company, 1977.

Sahakian, William S., *Ethics: An Introduction to Theories and Problems*. NY: Harper and Row, Publishers, 1974.

______________, *History of Philosophy*. NY: Harper and Row, Publishers, 1968.

______________, and Mabel L. Sahakian, *Ideas of the Great Philosophers*. NY: Harper and Row, Publishers, 1966.

Sartre, Jean-Paul, *Existentialism and Human Emotions*. NY: The Citadel Press, n.d.

Stumpf, Samuel Enoch, *Socrates to Sartre: A History of Philosophy*. NY: McGraw-Hill Book Company, 1966.

Thomas, Henry, *Understanding the Great Philosophers*. Garden City, NY: Doubleday and Company, Inc., 1962.

Tillich, Paul, *The Shaking of the Foundations*. NY: Charles Scribner's Sons, 1953.

Wild, John, *Existence and the World of Freedom*. Englewood Cliffs, NJ: Prentice-Hall, Inc., 1963.

Wilde, Jean T., and William Kimmel, eds. and trans., *The Search for Being*. NY: The Noonday Press, 1962.

Young, Warren C., *A Christian Approach to Philosophy*. Grand Rapids, MI: Baker Book House, 1954.

Have You Heard of the

Four Spiritual Laws?

1

Just as there are physical laws that govern the physical universe, so are there spiritual laws which govern your relationship with God.

LAW ONE

GOD **LOVES** YOU, AND OFFERS A WONDERFUL **PLAN** FOR YOUR LIFE.

(References contained in this booklet should be read in context from the Bible wherever possible.)

God's Love

"For God so loved the world, that He gave His only begotten Son, that whoever believes in Him should not perish, but have eternal life" (John 3:16).

God's Plan

(Christ speaking) "I came that they might have life, and might have it abundantly" (that it might be full and meaningful) (John 10:10).

Why is it that most people are not experiencing the abundant life? Because . . .

2

LAW TWO

MAN IS **SINFUL** AND **SEPARATED** FROM GOD. THEREFORE, HE CANNOT KNOW AND EXPERIENCE GOD'S LOVE AND PLAN FOR HIS LIFE.

Man Is Sinful

"For all have sinned and fall short of the glory of God" (Romans 3:23).

Man was created to have fellowship with God; but, because of his stubborn self-will, he chose to go his own independent way and fellowship with God was broken. This self-will, characterized by an attitude of active rebellion or passive indifference, is evidence of what the Bible calls sin.

Man Is Separated

"For the wages of sin is death" (spiritual separation from God) (Romans 6:23).

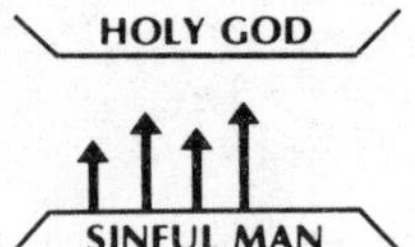

This diagram illustrates that God is holy and man is sinful. A great gulf separates the two. The arrows illustrate that man is continually trying to reach God and the abundant life through his own efforts, such as a good life, philosophy or religion.

The third law explains the only way to bridge this gulf . . .

3

LAW THREE

JESUS CHRIST IS GOD'S **ONLY** PROVISION FOR MAN'S SIN. THROUGH HIM YOU CAN KNOW AND EXPERIENCE GOD'S LOVE AND PLAN FOR YOUR LIFE.

He Died in Our Place

"But God demonstrates His own love toward us, in that while we were yet sinners, Christ died for us" (Romans 5:8).

He Rose from the Dead

"Christ died for our sins . . . He was buried . . . He was raised on the third day, according to the Scriptures . . . He appeared to Peter, then to the twelve. After that He appeared to more than five hundred . . ." (I Corinthians 15:3-6).

He Is the Only Way to God

"Jesus said to him, 'I am the way, and the truth, and the life; no one comes to the Father, but through Me' " (John 14:6).

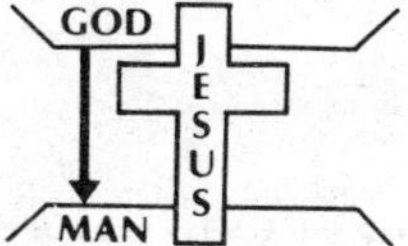

This diagram illustrates that God has bridged the gulf which separates us from Him by sending His Son, Jesus Christ, to die on the cross in our place to pay the penalty for our sins.

It is not enough just to know these three laws . . .

LAW FOUR

WE MUST INDIVIDUALLY **RECEIVE** JESUS CHRIST AS SAVIOR AND LORD; THEN WE CAN KNOW AND EXPERIENCE GOD'S LOVE AND PLAN FOR OUR LIVES.

We Must Receive Christ

"But as many as received Him, to them He gave the right to become children of God, even to those who believe in His name" (John 1:12).

We Receive Christ Through Faith

"For by grace you have been saved through faith; and that not of yourselves, it is the gift of God; not as a result of works, that no one should boast" (Ephesians 2:8,9).

When We Receive Christ, We Experience a New Birth. (Read John 3:1-8.)

We Receive Christ by Personal Invitation

(Christ is speaking): "Behold, I stand at the door and knock; if any one hears My voice and opens the door, I will come in to him" (Revelation 3:20).

Receiving Christ involves turning to God from self (repentance) and trusting Christ to come into our lives to forgive our sins and to make us the kind of people He wants us to be. Just to agree intellectually that Jesus Christ is the Son of God and that He died on the cross for our sins is not enough. Nor is it enough to have an emotional experience. We receive Jesus Christ by faith, as an act of the will.

These two circles represent two kinds of lives:

SELF-DIRECTED LIFE
S — Self is on the throne
† — Christ is outside the life
• — Interests are directed by self, often resulting in discord and frustration

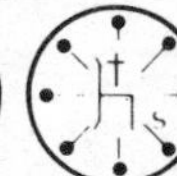

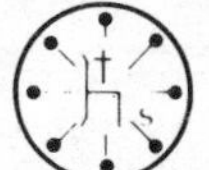

CHRIST-DIRECTED LIFE
† — Christ is in the life and on the throne
S — Self is yielding to Christ
• — Interests are directed by Christ, resulting in harmony with God's plan

Which circle best represents your life?

Which circle would you like to have represent your life?

The following explains how you can receive Christ:

YOU CAN RECEIVE CHRIST RIGHT NOW BY FAITH THROUGH PRAYER

(Prayer is talking with God)

God knows your heart and is not so concerned with your words as He is with the attitude of your heart. The following is a suggested prayer:

"Lord Jesus, I need You. Thank You for dying on the cross for my sins. I open the door of my life and receive You as my Savior and Lord. Thank You for forgiving my sins and giving me eternal life. Take control of the throne of my life. Make me the kind of person You want me to be."

Does this prayer express the desire of your heart?

If it does, pray this prayer right now, and Christ will come into your life, as He promised.

How to Know That Christ Is in Your Life

Did you receive Christ into your life? According to His promise in Revelation 3:20, where is Christ right now in relation to you? Christ said that He would come into your life. Would He mislead you? On what authority do you know that God has answered your prayer? (The trustworthiness of God Himself and His Word.)

The Bible Promises Eternal Life to All Who Receive Christ

"And the witness is this, that God has given us eternal life, and this life is in His Son. He who has the Son has the life; he who does not have the Son of God does not have the life. These things I have written to you who believe in the name of the Son of God, in order that you may know that you have eternal life" (I John 5:11-13).

Thank God often that Christ is in your life and that He will never leave you (Hebrews 13:5). You can know on the basis of His promise that Christ lives in you and that you have eternal life, from the very moment you invite Him in. He will not deceive you.

An important reminder . . .

DO NOT DEPEND UPON FEELINGS

The promise of God's Word, the Bible — not our feelings — is our authority. The Christian lives by faith (trust) in the trustworthiness of God Himself and His Word. This train diagram illustrates the relationship between **fact** (God and His Word), **faith** (our trust in God and His Word), and **feeling** (the result of our faith and obedience) (John 14:21).

The train will run with or without the caboose. However, it would be useless to attempt to pull the train by the caboose. In the same way, we, as Christians, do not depend on feelings or emotions, but we place our faith (trust) in the trustworthiness of God and the promises of His Word.

NOW THAT YOU HAVE RECEIVED CHRIST

The moment that you received Christ by faith, as an act of the will, many things happened, including the following:

1. Christ came into your life (Revelation 3:20 and Colossians 1:27).
2. Your sins were forgiven (Colossians 1:14).
3. You became a child of God (John 1:12).
4. You received eternal life (John 5:24).
5. You began the great adventure for which God created you (John 10:10; II Corinthians 5:17 and I Thessalonians 5:18).

Can you think of anything more wonderful that could happen to you than receiving Christ? Would you like to thank God in prayer right now for what He has done for you? By thanking God, you demonstrate your faith.

To enjoy your new life to the fullest . . .

SUGGESTIONS FOR CHRISTIAN GROWTH

Spiritual growth results from trusting Jesus Christ. "The righteous man shall live by faith" (Galatians 3:11). A life of faith will enable you to trust God increasingly with every detail of your life, and to practice the following:

G Go to God in prayer daily (John 15:7).

R Read God's Word daily (Acts 17:11)—begin with the Gospel of John.

O Obey God moment by moment (John 14:21).

W Witness for Christ by your life and words (Matthew 4:19; John 15:8).

T Trust God for every detail of your life (I Peter 5:7).

H Holy Spirit—allow Him to control and empower your daily life and witness (Galatians 5:16,17; Acts 1:8).

FELLOWSHIP IN A GOOD CHURCH

God's Word admonishes us not to forsake "the assembling of ourselves together. . ." (Hebrews 10:25). Several logs burn brightly together; but put one aside on the cold hearth and the fire goes out. So it is with your relationship to other Christians. If you do not belong to a church, do not wait to be invited. Take the initiative; call the pastor of a nearby church where Christ is honored and His Word is preached. Start this week, and make plans to attend regularly.

SPECIAL MATERIALS ARE AVAILABLE FOR CHRISTIAN GROWTH.

If you have come to know Christ personally through this presentation of the gospel, write for a free booklet especially written to assist you in your Christian growth.

A special Bible study series and an abundance of other helpful materials for Christian growth are also available. For additional information, please write Campus Crusade for Christ International, San Bernardino, CA 92414.

You will want to share this important discovery . . .